How To Sell
Travel Stories
Advice from editors

JAMES DURSTON

Do you travel to write, or do you write so you can travel?
No matter. No difference.

Just go.

CONTENTS

WWW.TRAVELWRITEEARN.COM

1 WHY I'M WRITING THIS BOOK

In the autumn of 2012 I was the senior producer and homepage editor for CNNGo, an online platform run by CNN for travel and lifestyle content. I was tasked with writing stories, assigning stories to freelancers, editing those stories and managing their publication on the site. Toward the back end of 2012 I received a pitch that in a roundabout way inspired this book. It wasn't the worst pitch I'd ever seen (we'll get to those later) in the same sense that a Chihuahua can't really be called the worst kind of dog. But it is a pretty regrettable dog. The conversation that followed this pitch went on for at least a half dozen emails and if you'll indulge me for a few pages, I'll dissect a little of it now.

Our wannabe travel writer was a freelance flight attendant for private jets. She already had a "successful blog" and now she wanted to "expand her audience" and so she got in touch. Would I like a story about her life in the air?

Ignoring a couple of typos, I responded.

Thanks for writing, I wrote back, I've taken a look at your blog and I'd be interested in discussing a story that's a little more specific than a generic account of your job. Do you have any particular ideas on some relevant themes you can send? Anything that can give our readers an inside glimpse of what it's like to be a VIP FA?

She replied, asking me to look deeper into her blog to see if there was anything I liked there. But I should bear in mind that she had to sign confidentiality papers that precluded her from discussing her clients.

Ok, I replied, again. Well, inside details are what we thrive on, so it really depends on what you're willing to divulge. Would you be willing to write about clients anecdotally without naming them? Or how about a piece: "7 reasons flight attendants have the best jobs in the world." That seems to suit your own perspective better, though like I say, it's the details that make a piece like that sing.

She responded again, with the following:

> On 5/9/12 9:44 PM, "*********@gmail.com"
> <*********@gmail.com>wrote:
>
> I was wondering what your thoughts were on
> the log I sent you. Andy earlier ones that were
> a bit more " racier"?

Log? Andy? A bit more racier?

After 15 years in the trade I can generally spot a typo before it bites me in the eye, but these made me wonder if I hadn't gotten mixed up in some strange email text-warp. Then I noticed there was an attachment. The "log." It was an attempt at "7 reasons flight attendants have the best jobs in the world." Except it was five. And it was terrible.

I politely declined her offer, vaguely identifying a couple of reasons, and quietly hoped that was the end of it. But within a few hours she responded, promising me another attempt to capture what I was looking for. And a few days later her name appeared in my inbox again, except it didn't come with an article, it came with a rather stinging criticism of a piece we had already run, that I had sent her as an example of what works well.

> On 19/9/12 4:59 AM, "* * * * * * * * *"
> <* * * * * * * * * *@gmail.com> wrote:
>
> ...it's just people bashing.. No class at all...if
> that is what you are looking for, than I
> defiantly can not produce that. If it is not, then
> you can give me a topic and I would be happy
> to produce an article for you. My blogs
> currently get great responses, imwas just
> looking to expand my audience.

Than? Defiantly? imwas?

My temper instantly corroded, my professionalism melted

away and I spent a good 30 minutes fashioning a response that I reproduce here in parts.

> On 19/9/12 2:59 PM, "James Durston"
> <**********> wrote:
>
> The fact that you are looking to "expand your audience" - something you have mentioned at least twice now – is about as relevant to me as the price of bras in Zimbabwe. I am not here to service your audience-expansion needs. I am here to provide my readers with excellent travel features.
>
> As a potential freelancer, you essentially have a product to sell (your stories). When you approach an editor, you are trying to make a sale. That is the relationship.
>
> If you are uncomfortable with my requests, fine, let me know and move on. But now you are also asking me to provide you with an idea. If I wanted to do that I may as well write the article myself.
>
> I am looking for articles that catch a reader unawares, or provide an enlightening insight into a part of life readers may not have previously considered. The article needs to generate a catchy headline and it needs to have shareability – people should be proud of sharing the article with their friends, whether

that's because it's funny or titillating or insightful or bizarre.

One final piece of advice - If you are serious about becoming a professional writer, it's always good to check your emails for typos and grammar before hitting send.

Hopefully these tips will stand you in good stead as you pitch stories elsewhere. I wish you the best of luck.

It's not a response I'm particularly proud of. The mature, more professional thing to have done, what the vast majority of editors do, is hit delete and move to the next item on the task list, consciously putting this writer's name on my personal "ignore list." But it was as if a dam had burst and all the years of bad-pitch-frustration were now spilling out of my head onto the keyboard.

For editors on the receiving end of pitches like these it's all too easy to click delete and never think about them again. Possibly, probably, I should have done just that. But that would achieve nothing. Feedback like mine here may sting, but if you're serious about writing and publishing, which she seemed to be, it'll also provide valuable information that should improve your chances of selling something later on. And as it happens, hers was just one of several Chihuahua pitches that would eventually prick me into a response.

Similar emails had been yapping their way into my inbox

with increasing frequency that year, writers appearing to consider the pitch an annoying inconvenience, a chore they need to go through but that really just wastes a bit more time before they can see their sparkling copy in print.

Unfortunately, without a good pitch you may as well have no story. There are some decent blog posts about pitching, but none goes far enough in my view. Because if you are "pitch perfect" for your target publication and target editor, you become a heavy green blip on the editorial radar. That's how this business works. No editor will ever refuse the perfect story. It may come with disclaimers - I can't assign it this month, it doesn't fit our schedule right now. But you will get the "yes" you need. Of course, once you file it can still be killed if it isn't up to scratch. But that's a tale for another book.

What this book won't tell you

This is the book you read after you've read the ones about how to travel on a shoestring, how to stay at hotels for free, what to do when you get diarrhea in a jungle and so on. I'm not going to tell you how to find an agent. I don't really intend to tell you how to write either, except when writing a pitch. I'm certainly not going to go on at length about how hard it is to be a travel writer or give you any hot tips for traveling on a freelance hack's budget. That's all been done before.

I will give some insight, in alternating chapters, about my life at CNNGo (which later became CNN Travel) and in Hong Kong. While not directly related to the advisory chapters, these insights into the lives of working editors, editorial executives and the goals and ambitions of platforms like CNN Travel, I hope will provide context that should help you understand with greater clarity some of the advice I give.

I'm going to assume you've planned or survived your trip and got a great idea; you're just not sure how to make it stand apart from the hundreds and thousands of other pitches raining into your chosen editor's inbox.

The most important thing I won't tell you is how to do all this from the writer's side of the send/receive button. There are hundreds of writers out there who have written books and/or blog posts, describing how they got to be successful. My idea is to do this from the other side of the email divide - the editor's side, to tell you what I'm thinking every time I get a pitch or assign a story, while also providing a few behind-the-scenes glimpses of how those thoughts were conceived and played out in the offices of CNNGo/CNN Travel in Hong Kong. These 'Inside CNN' insights will also give the bigger picture - describing the corporate goals and targets in our crosshair and how they affected the day-to-day work with content and freelancers.

One disclaimer: how I worked and assigned at CNN Travel is not how everyone assigns on every magazine or travel site. Some publications have assign-by-committee meetings every week to decide what's worth publishing months in advance of publication dates. Others, like CNN Travel, leave it up to individual editors to make sure their beat is covered as well as it can be. There will even be small differences between individual editors on the same publication. Just because I like an idea, doesn't mean my colleague will and, more importantly, doesn't mean my supervising editor will.

This is an important point that many writers would do well to understand: an assigning editor may be the last step on the journey for you, but your pitch is only part of the picture for us. We have our own managers - supervising editors, managing editors, executive editors and editorial directors, who in turn have their own general managers and other senior execs to answer to. Every time I assign a piece, I am also under scrutiny - do my tastes match those of my editor above me, am I on brand, on message, am I going to assign anything that could get us into trouble (yes, I did - see Chapter 14)? Especially important these days, does this content help or get us nearer to hitting sales and marketing targets?

So you could do everything I say and still not get commissioned. That's life. What I'm laying out here are some of the things you can do to give yourself the best chance. After all, the "don't give up" advice is bullshit. I've read at least two writers blogging about how to be a travel writer, regurgitating that tired, trite nonsense about persistence being the golden rule. Well, persistence and perseverance will actually count against you if you have a bad idea and a shitty pitch. So here's to making sure you have a great idea and an awesome golden retriever of a pitch.

2 INSIDE CNN: MONSOON EDIT TEST

Thunder explodes like a rifle, rain pours from a charcoal sky, lightning flashes every ten seconds. The rain pounds on everything, its noise muffling not just other sounds, but my very thoughts. Palm trees caught by the squalls rock and twitch as if being pummeled with grenades. Through it all a river courses, deep, brown, heavy waves twisting and broiling. I view all this through my office window on the third floor of a nondescript building in the middle of Mumbai.

It's my third monsoon and this year the downpour seems particularly heavy. Beneath the river is in fact a road that's now unusable. People who absolutely must walk through the torrent, trousers rolled above the knees, shoes in hand. Umbrellas have been discarded. They're useless against this barrage.

I'm two years into a managing editor role for a new B2B publishing company and have successfully launched six print titles for the Indian market. Which means the sales and business guys are ready to jump down my throat.

"Hey James, we sold a full page to Hafele, can you do a half page story?" asks Bibhor, the ad sales director. An air-conditioner rattles overhead. In the trash bin is a piece of glue paper stuck to which is a dead rat, caught that morning. Its sneering yellow teeth are marked with blood where the office peon cracked it with a shoe. I decide here, now, to look for another job.

Now it's October and it's raining again, this year's monsoon in its death throes, fitfully spluttering out single days of rain. I'm in Goa, a solo trip for a few days. The palm trees here feel altogether more at ease with the watery, windy battering, dancing rather than fighting. The landscape is verdant and fresh. I'm putting the finishing touches to an edit test for the role of copy editor at a new travel venture CNN has just launched. The usual kind of thing: edit this story, write these headlines, provide five story ideas, how would you tweet this? Helpfully (stupidly?), the stories I've been sent to edit are all published on CNN already. I compare their edited versions with mine, tweak mine where I think theirs is better, but not so much that it's obvious, and hit send.

The recruitment process up to this point, and beyond, is scattered. It goes something like this:

1. See ad: "Rock star deputy editor required" for CNNGo on Yahoo jobs site. Apply.
2. Wait a couple weeks with no response, so check the CNNGo website and sign up for the newsletter, when I will be informed of its launch.
3. A couple weeks later receive email that the site is launched. It includes an invitation to send

feedback on the site. Instead, I send a polite request asking if any decision has been made about the deputy editor role.

4. I quickly receive a response from the managing director of CNNGo that my application was not received, could I send again. I do so.

5. Three more weeks go by.

6. I send an email directly to the managing director again asking if any decision has been made, and by the way, here are some great ideas that I think could turn CNNGo into "Asia's most dynamic, must-visit Travel-Info site."

7. I receive an immediate reply: "I am sorry you haven't heard from us. We are days away from launch and up to our eyeballs in last minute tweaks. We promise to be in touch next week. Do reach out again if you don't hear back. God only knows what whackamoles will pop up once we are live."

8. I feel encouraged.

9. Two more weeks go by.

10. Another week goes by.

11. Days upon days, interminable in their silence, go by. Meanwhile two more rats have been caught in my office in Mumbai.

12. I try to call. No response.

13. I write again, and attach an article for them to use, should they like it: A guide to Mumbai's noises. "City of dins."

14. Two days later a response comes from the editor in chief offering me some freelance work instead. I sigh, assuming this means the full-time job is off

the table, say ok thanks, sure put me in touch with your Mumbai editor. The dead rats keep grinning.

15. Two days later the EIC writes again, asking if I can do some edit tests "that aren't really edit tests, more a collection of ideas," and also edit some bad copy as a proper edit test and also have a chat some time.

16. Encouraged again, I write back immediately, saying yes to everything, I will basically be your slave if you help me escape these dead rats.

17. Great, will send tomorrow, he writes back.

18. Tomorrow comes and goes.

19. But the day after a big fat edit test lands in my inbox and I'm encouraged once again. Now all I have to do is pass the test.

20. I send back the test.

21. A week goes by.

22. A couple more days go by, and I decide to put the pressure on. My visa is expiring in India, my apartment contract needs to be renewed - have I got the job or not?

23. He responds: "James – hi. Got your note about rent etc. I'll be honest with you...."

24. Oh great.

25. "We like a couple of other candidates for the Dep Ed that we are chasing … But I do need a copy/sub ed. Not sure what sort of $ you are on now or that sort of appeal, but is that something that interests you and you could step right into now? If I had a copy ed/subbie that was inspired to do more than just that, that would be a bonus."

26. The rats. They grin.

27. I respond, making sure to sound disappointed (I'm a managing editor for shit's sake) but ok, what are the details?

I'll spare you the full rundown but basically after a full 72 emails from start to end, several phone calls, an edit test and various extracurricular offerings from myself, I landed in Hong Kong with my life in two suitcases and a new job title - copy editor, CNNGo. The future was less ratty, much more neon.

3 THE BEST PITCH I EVER RECEIVED

So what would a perfect pitch look like? Inevitably every editor around the world has his or her own preferences. Here I'll lay out how I request pitches come to me. I think most editors would agree that the format I'll describe makes it quick and easy to decide whether the story is right for their publication or not. That's really what a good pitch is all about.

It's staggering to me that in a decade of assigning content, I've only once received a pitch that landed in this format without my requesting it first. I have the author's permission to show you that pitch - the best I've ever received - which I've pasted at the end of this chapter.

In my idyllic editorial world, the perfect pitch would look like this:

Headline

50-word summary

More info (100 words)

Imagery

This succinctly lays out what the story is about and allows me to quickly judge whether it's something I (and my readers) might be interested in. But beyond this the perfect pitch would have one quality - I wouldn't need to change a thing or ask any questions. And, hopefully, when the piece arrived, I wouldn't make a single edit or source a single image, and could immediately load the thing into the content management system and hit publish. That's what editors dream of and what writers should aspire to.

Reality is never so glitch-free and even when I get pitches in line with the above, it's rare I'll assign immediately without at least a little discussion about the main theme or angle of the piece, ask some questions about fact sourcing, possible interviews and so on. But the recipe above is a good clean start, and here's why.

Headline

Journalism courses pre-Internet always taught that the headline should be the last thing you write, once you've written the story and actually know what it's about. Many writers that file to me don't bother with even a cursory attempt at a headline, probably assuming that the sub-editors or I have that covered.

That's the first mistake you can make in a pitch to an

online publication. Firstly, it's rare these days that an online publication, unless it's huge, will have a team of sub-editors. The journalism profession has undergone a bundling of roles, where the writer is the editor and often the photographer or at least the photo-researcher too, as well as the Facebooker, Tweeter, search-engine-optimizer and coffee-getter. The headline is, for an Internet story, also a pitch to the reader: read this! You cannot not click this story! Miss this and you miss out! It only takes a few seconds' thought to see why the Internet requires us to flip the old school headline lesson on its head.

Flicking through a magazine or newspaper, your reader is held captive, eyes scanning maybe three or four headlines in the news section, down to one headline over up to eight pages in the features well. Competition between stories here is tiny to non-existent. There is context everywhere - pictures, captions and other snippets of text will all provide information to the reader about the article in attractive formats. And for that reason, you'll sometimes see feature headlines in a hardcopy magazine that tell you nothing about the story you might be about to read. Forefront is style, or a clever pun (I hate puns), or some graphic flourish. So "Truly, Madly, Deeply" (I also hate film title headlines) becomes a headline for a story about a love affair between two psychiatrists. "The Dark Knight" becomes a headline for a winemaker who makes wine in the depths of a cave.

If online writers construct headlines like this, their stories die, quickly. Scan a content-heavy website and you may have up to a hundred stories crammed together, bumping and overlapping and jostling for the reader's attention.

There are few or no contextual add-ons. The stories that get the traffic are promoted and propped up so they can get even more traffic, the stories that no one reads are quickly removed from the front pages, relegated to the bottomless abyss of "the archive." CNN in the United States has hourly traffic targets and anything that isn't pulling its weight is swiftly replaced. This survival of the fittest style of programming a site doesn't depend entirely on the headline, but it plays a key role in making readers decide to click or not.

It's said that 80% of people read headlines and just 20% read the story. So how do we convert browsers into readers? What makes for a good headline online? There's no single formula you should follow each time you write a head. Different stories will require different treatments and good headline writing is as much a craft as good writing is, even in the Internet age. But say my editor said to me one morning, "We're going to be 100,000 clicks short of our target this month - I need you to get a story up that'll cover that shortfall over the next 24 hours." In this case, which is perfectly possible in online publishing, my go-to formula for a headline that I know will generate above average clicks would look something like this:

Number + superlative + thing + place = clicks

Yes, that's a list. Scream all you want about lists being the editorial equivalent of a deep-fried pizza - I'm here to tell you what works in the minds of traffic-needy editors, and lists work. For psychological reasons that have been explored and interpreted in multifarious articles, Internet users love to click a list. And given that most, if not all online editors have traffic targets, lists are an easy option to keep traffic high. Here are the headlines for some of my high-traffic assigns while at CNN:

World's 50 most delicious foods

20 of the world's most iconic skyscrapers

World's 100 best beaches

27 sights that will remind you how incredible Earth is

Asia's 10 greatest street food cities

10 things Italy does better than anywhere else

World's happiest countries: 1 to 187

15 unusual places to spend a night

19 greatest bonus-busting experiences

10 most beautiful university buildings

I've selected these because they fit the formula I describe above and because they were commissions I personally made. They're not the top ten stories from CNN Travel during my tenure there. But a glance at the top stories over a period shows that the general rule above holds for most of the top stories by pageview. Below is a snapshot of the top 20 stories published by CNNGo up to November 2012 (when CNNGo was disbanded and merged into the wider CNN website as CNN Travel):

	Page
1.	Home
2.	World's 50 most delicious foods
3.	The world's coolest nationalities: Where do you rank?
4.	http://www.cnngo.com
5.	Shanghai city
6.	Asia's most sinful cities
7.	20 of the world's most iconic skyscrapers
8.	Hong Kong city
9.	World's 50 best beaches
10.	America's most sinful cities
11.	Tokyo city
12.	10 of the world's most hated airports
13.	Bangkok city
14.	7 sexy skinny dips
15.	Singapore city
16.	World's 50 most delicious drinks
17.	World's 12 worst tourist traps
18.	Seoul city
19.	40 Taiwanese foods we can't live without
20.	World's sexiest accents

Excepting the home and city landing pages (1, 4, 5, 8, 11, 13, 15, 18), every one of these follows the rule to some extent. Numbers (50, 20, 10...), superlatives (most delicious, coolest, most sinful, most iconic, best...), things (foods, cities, skyscrapers, beaches...) and places (world, America, Asia, Taiwan...). At the time of recording (November 2012) the top 14 stories here all had pageviews in excess of 1 million. They will all have a lot more too by now (November 2016).

"But wait," I hear you think. "This book is meant for

travel writers - are these strictly travel stories? Are lists of sinful cities and sexy accents now game for travel pitches?"

This is slightly off topic for this chapter, but let me give a quick answer just to quench your curiosity: those pieces fit for CNNGo. Which is why good writers research the publication they want to pitch, before pitching. I will concede my supervising editor and I struggled a little with the "America's sinful cities" idea, especially considering the furor that erupted when we published Asia's most sinful cities. See Chapter 14 for an entertaining tale about that piece. What swayed us was the knowledge that a) we had a great writer doing the American version whom we knew would write it brilliantly, research it thoroughly and be highly entertaining, and b) it would get huge traffic.

That's not to say all stories likely to get a million hits are a guaranteed commission, nor is it to say high-traffic lists are the only stories worth considering. But in a 50-50 situation they may help your idea fall on the positive side of that line.

Take another look at that snapshot of the top stories above and you may notice a dilemma for you as a travel writer. These are clearly not the kinds of stories you write having just gone somewhere or done something. Most lists like these are exercises in creative research, "desk writes" as I call them, that can be done with a Google connection and a couple of spare evenings. Sure you could at least part-fund your three-night beach excursion with a few pieces like this, but that's hardly the same as traveling to Bali as a travel writer to write about Bali is it? Chapter 9 goes into this in more depth, but it's worth asking yourself what kind of writer you are, or want to be, or are happy to be. That can define, or at least guide, your story ideas and your pitches.

Other kinds of headline

No one wants to write or read lists all day, every day. Some don't want to write lists at all, any day. I, as a list-hungry editor, think those who avoid or refuse to consider lists among their oeuvre are needlessly skipping by piles of easy cash, albeit small piles. Younger writers don't seem to have this problem. Lists are a major part of the media they consume, and so it's natural they'll fit into the landscape of their work. It seems to be older writers who feel that lists in some way are a corruption of their craft. And I do hear you. A website full of nothing but lists is like a banquet table covered in nothing but desserts. Tasty, for a while, but hardly nutritious. Which is why traditional feature stories remain important to many travel websites.

So what's the formula to a non-list headline? There isn't one and I won't try to reduce this entire art to something mathematical. But I will still argue that in order to sell your story, you need to be thinking about the headline from the outset. So if your story's about the fishermen of Inle Lake in Myanmar, what's going to really sell the piece to your editor? Don't forget, in turn, he or she will be thinking about how to sell this piece to their managers and eventually readers. What's unique or special or enthralling or gripping about your story? What's the miss-it-miss-out quality? Here are some categories of headline that can at least frame your story idea. Each example headline is a real story that I assigned (and in most cases probably wrote the headline for too) or is a real story I saw on the Internet and liked.

The thing that it is

Some stories are their own headlines. To try to embellish these is not only unnecessary, it may even detract from the essence and intrigue of the piece.

Gallery: Myanmar's leg rowers of Inle Lake

Vietnam's farmer violinists

The sulfur slaves of Kawah Ijen

Riding shotgun in the Gumball 3000

The people who create their own "countries"

First person

Travel writing in its purest form is a description of an experience with the thoughts and personal interpretations that come to the writer during a trip. First-person headlines underline this connection between the writer, the experience and the reader.

Why I climb insanely tall buildings with my bare hands

Why I hope to die at 75

How I got over my fear of flying

The drink that nearly knocked me out with one sniff

SEO

Search engine optimization - modifying content to match what people search for - is the steamed cauliflower on our editorial plates. We know it's good for us, but it's just so yucky. Entire books and thousands, possibly millions of blog and web posts have been written about editorial attempts to second-guess Google. I'm not going to even touch it here, except to say that SEO-derived headlines, and indeed story ideas, can and do work. I even once assigned a story based on the top Google searches for travel: "Time travel with your cat: How Google sees your vacation plans."

Best French restaurants in Paris

Where is Okinawa?

Where to get married: World's best wedding venues

How tos

This kind of headline requires a certain type of article and in many cases they're a subset of the SEO category. If the idea is good, these headlines can be highly clickable.

How to take better travel photos

How to fly first-class for free

How to be a Hong Kong local: 10 tips for faking it (ok a how to-list combo)

How to become a Bollywood extra

Teasers

The teaser headline can often be considered click-baity and

annoying. But if you're not gratuitous about it, they can work.

The world's best airport is ...

Possibly the year's greatest travel photo

World's happiest country is where?

Questions

Old-school journos will say, "You're not writing articles to ask questions, you're writing articles to answer them." But nothing gets to the heart of an angle like the question you probably asked when the idea came to you.

What's it like to be crucified?

Is massage good for you or does it just feel nice?

Is this the inventor of bubble tea?

What's life like in paradise?

Do you care if your hotel has good art?

As I write these I realize this list of headline categories could go on for a few pages. Which underlines the point that there is no formula. The trick, the craft, the art and the science of a good headline has to come from your idea of what the most important or interesting aspect of the story is. And how can you boil that down to eight or ten words, in the style of your chosen publication?

I consider the headline the absolute key component of your pitch. If I like it, I'll certainly read on. A good headline that sums up the story and also fits the voice and style of my publication gives me confidence that you know what you're doing, that you're a proper pro who understands the nature of this business and working with you may not just be good for the site and for our readers (and by extension myself) but could be the start of an ongoing relationship that makes my job a lot easier and more enjoyable.

Now comes the disclaimer: unless you're writing a list and follow the headline formula described above, your headline probably won't make it onto the published page. Editors, simply through years of experience, will have a much better feel for what their publication needs and each editor will have their own personal preferences to boot. But that's not your concern. You're concerned with selling a story. What happens after that is out of your hands. Your headline is designed to sell your story to your editor. And that's as far as you should plan.

A good headline is an introduction. You need to back it up with meaningful information about the story itself. If the headline is a doorway, you also need to describe the room - at least the basic furnishings. You can think of your pitch as a micro-version of a feature. The best online content has a great, clickable headline, and then backs it up with superb content. The headline pulls you in, the story gets it shared. And the instant you back up your possibly clickbait headline with good content, it ceases to be clickbait and becomes a great article. A successful story fulfills the promise of its headline. And the best pitches back up their working headlines with great summaries.

So now to the best pitch I ever received, from a freelance travel writer named Richard Mellor. This was not right for my publication at the time, so I declined the story, but I know he did soon sell it to the Independent On Sunday and also Passport, Monarch Airline's in-flight magazine.

After connecting with me on LinkedIn, here's what he wrote:

> Hi James,
>
> Thanks for connecting with me, much appreciated. Reading about LE PAN made me realize my forthcoming trip, next week, is very relevant. I'm not sure if you're the person to whom I should pitch, but here goes anyway:
>
> ### GRUB WITH THE GRAPES – BORDEAUX'S FOOD REVOLUTION
>
> Sell: Gordon Ramsay's arrival clinches it: the old wine city has become a new food city
>
> With his just-opened Pressoir-d'Argent, Gordon Ramsay joins Joel Robuchon and Philippe Etchebest, host of the French version of Kitchen Nightmares, in recently opening in Bordeaux. Throw in Miles, co-winner of Gallic bible Le Fooding's recent Restaurant of the Year award, and the old wine city has suddenly become a new food city.
>
> Other reasons to visit are much-improved

museums, a once-crummy riverside made pretty again and, of course, those grand cru vineyards. There's also a 'go now' imperative, before lads and luddites arrive: Bordeaux is a host-city for summer's Euro 2016 international football tournament, while 2017 will see the completion of a high-speed TGV line from Paris.

I've been invited on a press trip to visit Bordeaux and Pressoir-d'Argent next week.

Hope this might work. Please feel free to email me on ricardo.mellor@gmail.com (I can explain...!) if it does.

All my best,

Richard

Great headline, great sell, good extra details, good research into my publication, succinct and timely. There's no way to improve this.

4 INSIDE CNN: LANDING
IN HONG KONG

Wheel screech. Tire smoke. Busy airport. Shitty hotel. Neon lights. Smoky bars. Beers, cocktails, girls, maybe some drugs, more girls, get in a fight, pass out on the floor of some triad king's brothel. That would be Guy Ritchie's version of my Hong Kong arrival montage.

This is my version: Wheel screech. Tire smoke. Calm airport. Nice taxi. Perfectly decent hotel. Great power shower. Call my girlfriend. Sleep.

I arrive and spend 24 non-outrageous hours acquainting myself with my new home. These days are exhilarating, nonetheless. Few things can provide the skin-prickling, gut-warming thrill of landing in a new city with no return ticket. It's actually physiological, that feeling, as if your biology is preparing to enter the fight-or-flight response, but is just holding back, teetering on the edge of a huge adrenaline shot. As it happens, flying or fighting were the last things to cross my mind during a comparatively blissful Honky introduction.

The differences with India are stark.

We've seen how India handles the monsoon - it doesn't. In Hong Kong, I witness a light rain burst being rendered impotent with two dozen small sandbags, channeling water away from the walkway, leaving a central dry passage for pedestrians.

Here, people queue. In India, people charge, following one rule: "me" getting there first, which applies to everyone. I walk to the CNN office for the first time to see a single-file line at least 20 meters long outside the elevator lobby. People quietly, patiently waiting. I suppress an urge after years of Indian life to saunter past the crowd and stand directly outside the elevator doors like I own them. I join the queue and feel like Crocodile Dundee in New York.

And the taxis. My cab to Mumbai airport is modeled on the much-revered Hindustan Ambassador, a smooth, rolling ride of comfort and indulgence. But my cab appears to have been banged together in a potting shed. The doors don't clunk, they clang. The "air-conditioning" comes through natural worn holes in the rusting floor - I watch the road zipping by as we drive. And the roof is about 12 inches too low. I get out of the contraption after the 30-minute journey and have a crick in my neck that stays with me for three days.

Hong Kong's Toyota Crown Comforts are possibly the best taxis in the world. There are better cars out there - you'd have to give the award for Most Indulgent Ride to Moscow's Porsches. And London's black cabs are spacious, agile and driven by the most knowledgeable taxi drivers of all (especially if you ask them about politics). But considering all qualities desirable in a cab - availability, road knowledge, cleanliness, safety and price - none can challenge Hong Kong's red chariots. I'm shocked when I don't have to haggle for ten minutes before getting inside the cab (in Delhi, every single auto-rickshaw or cab ride is preceded by a discussion over price, due to the fact that every single fare meter in the city is "broken.")

I'm alarmed when I say the name of my hotel, and without a word the ride starts, as if he knows exactly where he's going. The real shocker? He does. The car has seat belts and heaters that actually work, my clothes and skin don't stick to the seat and the 30-minute journey costs just 40 U.S. bucks. This is too good to be true, I think. But seven years later I stand by it - Hong Kong's taxis are a benchmark for all cabs around the world.

Over the next few days I wander the streets in Central surprised to see how many other white folk there are. In India "goras" take to the streets knowing they'll almost certainly be the only Westerner in sight - the attention you get gives you a rough sense of what celebrity must feel like elsewhere. Hong Kong's throngs of Brit, Aussie and French "gweilo" are something I'm not prepared for - I feel a pang of disappointment knowing I'm no longer a rare object.

Of course it's silly to compare these two cities in any kind of judgmental way. I enjoyed the chaos of India and the sense of freedom that comes with. Moving from one to the other is like moving from a sweaty cabaret show in Bangkok to a Verdi opera in Geneva. Both enjoyable and worthwhile, in their own ways.

*

TALKING EDS

Monica Drake, travel editor, New York Times

Worst pitch?

I don't know about the worst pitch but I would say that pitches that make it clear that nobody has ever read our coverage are frustrating. Also the "I'm traveling to xx if you want a story from there" pitch is a common pitfall for freelancers. We have a staff of reporters all over the world, so if we want a story from any destination, chances are, we can dispatch someone. I'd recommend doing research and coming up with a story idea of your own.

Perfect pitch?

I have received pitches that stand out because they mention things that I'm interested in. Also pitches that are pretty straightforward are all good. Writers should be able to almost write a headline and just a few sentences about the angle.

Assigns?

The pitches that I assign generally offer a new perspective on a familiar destination or a really interesting destination that is far flung and going through a change. Some examples of the latter are this piece on the Canary Islands and this one on the Arctic Circle.
URLs:
http://www.nytimes.com/2016/05/08/travel/canary-islands-astronomy-stargazing.html
http://www.nytimes.com/2016/02/14/travel/canada-tuk-northwest-territory.html

Writing goals?

I generally edit, not write. When I do write, it's often a personal piece, like this one on <u>being born on Sept. 11</u> or this one on <u>skiing with my daughter.</u>

URLs:

http://cityroom.blogs.nytimes.com/2008/09/10/a-celebration-albeit-a-delicate-one/

http://www.nytimes.com/2015/12/13/travel/skiing-children-new-hampshire.html.

5 THE WORST PITCH
I EVER RECEIVED

There were several recurring conversation topics in the CNN Travel office, among them music (and how everyone other than the speaker had bad taste), food (and how Chinese women invented "hangry" years before it became a meme), interns (and where they ranked on the cute/annoying/crapness scales), internal CNN politics (and how lucky we were that at least one of us played these games expertly) and of course, freelancers.

Discussions over freelancers varied but usually referred to either a plea for more money, or a plea to re-edit their text, or a plea simply for a reply. The most enjoyable discussions centered on the terrible pitches we would receive, sometimes daily.

I've taken the liberty, without naming anyone, of listing the

Top 5 Terrible Pitches I can remember receiving since becoming an editor.

5. The way-too-wordy pitch

I received a pitch from a writer I knew only from LinkedIn that ran to 1,082 words. The pitch covered four or five story angles, but they blended into each other like forgotten dreams and had none of the structure I outlined in Chapter 3. She even offered to flesh them out if I was interested and followed up two hours later with a 300-word addendum.

If you're going to send extensive pitches with multiple angles or story ideas they need to be structured with at-a-glance signposts such as headlines and sub-heads (standfirsts or deks) that allow me to quickly gauge their value. I'd still argue that sending 1,400 words for an article that may only run to 800 is a mistake.

4. The you're-so-bad-you-need-me pitch

I received a pitch that went: "Should you wish at some point to pull out of the direction you look to be embracing and actually publish some decent content rather than the questionable stuff you've been doing recently, I can provide."

Any editor's reaction to this kind of note will be to scoff and publicly declare this writer blacklisted, for now. Editors are human and do need to be kicked up the ass sometimes, but this should come from their own editors, not freelancers trying to sell them stories.

In this note, this writer a) called into question the editor's judgment and professionalism (why would you want to write for someone whose work you don't respect?) and b) didn't even pitch anything, merely mentioned they could pitch in future.

That said, one editor bemused me recently when she admitted that when a PR mentioned she had spelt the name of the key product in her article wrong, she consciously decided never to write anything that PR sent again. That was over-sensitive. But many editors do consider these kinds of comments attacks on their talent and for that reason it's wise to be diplomatic.

3. The help-me-expand-my-audience pitch

The dented and slightly greening bronze medal for worst pitch I ever got goes to the writer who inspired the opening chapter of this book. Yes, we met this particular blogging flight attendant in Chapter 1. We know this tale. A pitch that focuses primarily on the benefit to the writer is going nowhere slow, even if it is jet powered.

2. The way-out-of-my-depth pitch

Two faux-silver medals made in China for 1) the young writer from India who pitched me a story about "10 things you always need to do before traveling" and 2) a writer from the UK who pitched me a story about "Great social tools for travelers." We have a tie for this second spot, both pitches suffering the same lackluster illness.

The first was a headline with potential. The first hurdle was jumped and I was led to expect (hope for) a fresh or funny take on what would otherwise be a shoulder-shrug of a piece. Then the pitch immediately collapsed. There was nothing fresh or funny or even interesting to follow. In truth, this wasn't so much a problem with the pitch as it was the very concept of the story she proposed. She had gone to the trouble of listing out in brief form all ten of the items, and they included such gems as: "Check your passport is valid;" "Remember to get a visa;" "Pack light;" "Do some research." Not bad advice - for a teenager going on his or her first trip outside the country. But redundant and downright dumb for an audience with any sophistication. This was a good example of a story that wouldn't fulfill the promise of its headline.

The second I unfortunately don't have recourse to, having deleted it immediately, and no doubt with a face like a pug chewing mud. But having promised what I assumed would be a list of social tools and networks targeted specifically at travelers, instead I was recommended to use the biggest, most obvious social tools in existence: Facebook, Instagram and a new thing called Vine.

If your pitch is that predictable, so will be my response.

1. The bone-idle pitch

If I could personally send dozens of crumpled gold-paper medals to the dozens of freelancers who commit this pitching crime every month, I still would not, because that would involve effort on my part, and this worst pitch of all time is a lesson in unadulterated laziness.

The pitch comes in various forms, but all are kin to this basic idea: "Hi James, I'm going to [Cambodia] next month, do you want a story?"

Insert your own city/country/landmass. A few weeks ago this offense spread to an entire continent: "Hi James, I've arranged a trip to Africa in a few weeks and just wanted to check if you needed anything from there?"

When I get pitches like this, I feel how a diner would feel if he sits down at a top restaurant and is presented with a menu that lists a single item: "Food".

At first glance you may think I'm being petty. What's wrong with this simple enquiry? It may come to nothing, but should I be running a 12-week series on African Adventures, you've hit the mother lode, right? Well, possibly, but the chances of that are lottery-like and it's still inexcusably lazy, which will annoy me enough to decide not to assign to you.

A pitch is not a pitch unless it contains details of your story, an angle or a theme or an idea - something to intrigue me, maybe even fill me with excitement and anticipation.

One retort to this kind of pitch that came to me courtesy Chuck Thompson, CNN Travel's executive editor, and came to him courtesy one of his former editors, goes thus: [Cambodia] is a place, not a story idea.

That simple line goes a long way to describing what editors look for in pitches.

6 INSIDE CNN: MY BOSS,
THE 'FUCKHEAD'

I wake up, mouth feeling like an open wound, head throbbing, eyes stinging. Someone groans like a dying sloth. I realize it's me. I'm in my hotel room. Good. I see my wallet and phone. Excellent. I check my text messages. Nothing. I click to the Sent folder. Something. Oh god. Oh Jesus god.

Christmas Day starts at noon in the Foreign Correspondents' Club, a popular hangout for journos and writers in Hong Kong. My new boss and CNNGo's editor in chief Andrew Demaria kindly invites me along to his Christmas Day lunch with his girlfriend and friends, knowing I'm alone just a couple of weeks into a new city. There's wine and Champagne and beer, and we drink it all, chased down with the occasional bite of food.

For me the day's not only a Christmas party but also a celebration of my new life here as a member of this huge, international news brand and how I've slotted into the team and found a rhythm. Hong Kong is awesome, working at CNN is great, life is good.

My first week passes fast. HR induction, colleague introductions, work. The emphasis right now is on volume - pumping out six to eight pieces of content a day split between short "re-blogs" and longer features. The office is quiet - each staff focused on their monitor - but the feel is nonetheless one of a startup. A regular office space with desk dividers, but it's nearly empty. The CNNGo staff number around ten in a space that could probably fit sixty. Small teams aren't new to me, but the hushed stillness and near silence that sometimes descends is. There's a small kitchen area with microwave, tea and coffee. I glimpse a majestic view across Hong Kong Harbour through a row of doored-off offices at the back.

My induction involves a quick overview of the site - my first proper glimpse into the structure and editorial strategy those already here have established. CNNGo is an English-language website focused on six Asian cities - Bangkok, Hong Kong, Mumbai, Shanghai, Singapore and Tokyo - each city with its own dedicated page, editor and freelance budget. There's also a homepage editor whose job is to manage the content flowing in from the city editors as well as write and assign content that doesn't fit the locale-specific niches of the city pages. This role becomes mine in a year's time. There's the copy editor (me). Two further roles complete the editorial lineup - an editorial director who oversees all city and homepage content and strategy and above him the editor in chief. The site's tagline is "Local insights. Global experiences".

I immediately get down to editing content. Each of the

six to eight pieces that we publish has to pass through me, the copy editor, after a first edit from the assigning editor. I then pass it back to the editor who takes care of publication. Associate editor Chris Anderson takes care of homepage content and is my desk neighbor and handholder for the first few days. He's a friendly-faced, dark-haired Californian, more of a nerdy web surfer than an ocean surfer, and we hit it off. We're soon out drinking beers, shooting pool and meeting girls in Hong Kong's bar areas.

Our relationship sours about a year later when I send an email to him and copy in a bunch of other edit staff about an article he edited poorly. When he's let go in the first of CNNGo's two redundancy pushes and I step into his place, he seems to think I played a role in his fate, asking me via email several months later what I know about his termination. As it happens I know no more than he does. But until that point we're buddies.

My neighbor on the other side is Jordan Burchette, deputy editor, blonde, bright-eyed, immaculately presented Floridian, former executive editor of Maxim.com and a sharp wit. Burchette is my desk neighbor for only a few months before he leaves for New York, but I like him - in the same way you like a stand-up comic. He's entertaining and makes your day more fun, but you know when he speaks he does so for all in earshot, not just for you.

MunYin Liu is the social media and marketing guy. MunYin is an instantly likeable, energized British-born Chinese guy who's one of the first to send me a welcome message on Skype, the communication channel of choice for CNNGo. He's obsessed with PG Tips tea, and asks whether, as a fellow Brit, I happen to have any with me.

Brent Deverman is product manager. Brent I learn to like a lot as the years go on. His droning tone - the subject of a few jokes over the years ("if I ever get insomnia I'll just record Brent talking") - belies an astonishing drive and energy - as well as running the technical side of CNNGo full time he runs his own website business in China (where he also lives - commuting three to four hours every day) as well as a monthly cheese and wine event. He's also the only purebred Westerner on the team able to communicate in Putonghua.

Efren Macasaet, web developer. A Filipino charmer whose love of chatting up the ladies comes second only to the love he showers on himself, Efren joins a couple months after me. His near daily reminders to the girls in the office that he's "MBA" - Married But Available - are somehow charming rather than obnoxious.

Zoe Li, Hong Kong editor. A Hong Kong Canadian, Li is aloof and rather too icy cool to be approachable. I share maybe ten words with her the first week. Li's the ringleader of a girly clique she forms with two junior writers, Tiffany Lam and Virginia Lau, all of them addicted to food and some actor called Andy Lau. I later learn he's Hong Kong's equivalent of Brad Pitt.

Kim Willis, general manager. A fiery, forty-something unmarried marketing pro from Oklahoma, I feel indebted to Willis for supporting my application, for agreeing to cover my travel and first month's accommodation expenses and for agreeing to a salary lift I negotiated. But I soon hear tales of her butting heads with a former editorial director who does not renew his six-month contract, likely a result of her. During a CNN internal staff review, in which managers are "reviewed" by their underlings, one of

CNNGo's junior writers writes something to the effect of: "I suggest Kim seeks the help and advice from loved ones or professionals." This staffer no doubt thinks she's being helpful. But it's a telling observation that would not have been lost on the senior execs. Willis is later released from the project.

I'm introduced over Skype to the team of editors spread around Asia: Sita Wadhwani, Mumbai editor, who becomes my flirt buddy. W. David Marx, Tokyo editor, who I never meet nor talk directly to. Larry Loh, Singapore editor, whose ebullient nature disguises a slipshod organizational ability that is only revealed when he leaves and I take over his role for a month. Lovely guy though. Jessica Beaton, Shanghai editor, possibly the worst copy editor I've ever known in a senior role. Lovely girl though. Karla Cripps, Bangkok editor, Canuck, drinker, smoker, pool-player, mother. KC (another CNN habit I quickly pick up - calling people by their initials) is everyone's best friend and one of our more competent reporter-editors.

And of course there's Andrew Demaria, editor in chief. I have a fairly good idea of what my new Australian boss will be like having exchanged dozens of emails and had several phone calls in the previous weeks and months. The real man matches my expectations perfectly. Laid back yet particular, gregarious but cool, "Demazepam" as I occasionally refer to him is a boss who becomes a buddy. My first day in the office I make a point to mention how a few months back England reclaimed the Ashes from Australia (that's cricket, for any non-Brit, non-Aussie readers), and he smirks.

And it's to him that the regrettable text messages I'm squinting at in a state of hung-over delirium on Boxing

Day 2009 have been sent.

Christmas lunch at the FCC ends around 5 pm. Demaria suggests we head to his place to continue the festivities (drinking) and my semi-sozzled rationale goes something like: sure, I've had food, I feel fine, and it's only 5 pm on Christmas Day. It would be rude not to accept my new boss's invitation to drink more at his house. A few hours, several beers and at least two extremely delicious but horrifyingly strong espresso martinis later, I leave Demaria's place (right after he kicks me out) and head back through the streets toward Central to find a cab to my hotel.

Perhaps it's because getting a cab on Christmas night is impossible. Or perhaps I didn't even contemplate that the night should end here and now. It's also unfortunate that between Demaria's place and my hotel lie most of Hong Kong's most hedonistic bars, including those in alcohol-fueled party district Lan Kwai Fong. But it's here that I spend US$50 on a club entry ticket, the only moment of which I can recall is sitting down on a seat and passing out.

So I find myself on Boxing Day morning 2009, squinting into my Sent messages to Demaria, praying I'm hallucinating. Or that someone stole my phone and it wasn't me that sent these. Or even that I stole someone else's phone and these aren't my messages at all. "It's only 10pm fuckhead - what am I supposed to do now?" reads the text.

Fuckhead. Oh Jesus. The fear runs through my veins like icy melt water.

Then I see another, inviting him for more beers in Lan Kwai Fong. There are no responses. It occurs to me that I might get sacked in the first month of this awesome job.

Later, Demaria reveals those text messages actually raised his level of respect for me. And that tells you all you need to know about the man.

So I become a part of this motley crew, a bit of circus act, in all truth, determined to create something important, but exactly what that is and how we'll accomplish it still seems to be up for debate.

And within 18 months several of the people mentioned above will have their contracts cut as Turner Broadcasting decides small is beautiful.

7 THE MIDDLE-CLASS, EMPTY-NESTER TRAVEL WRITER

Do all bored housewives eventually metamorphose into travel writers? Is being a bored housewife some kind of preparatory challenge, completion of which leads to the reward of being a wannabe travel writer?

Before I go much further, let me offer a disclaimer: this chapter is in no way meant to disparage or undermine the gallant work mothers and housewives do around the world, prior to the point they decide to become travel writers. If you want, you could argue that a life of traveling and writing is the least that should be awarded for the labors and sacrifices made during a housewife's years of toil. But you'd be taking me too literally.

I've been pitched and read articles by a 20-year-old female blogger and a 50-year-old male journalist - and they both projected into my head this image of a Chardonnay-sipping retiree on holiday who decides the thoughts s/he's penned into his/her journal sound rather nice actually and perhaps a travel magazine or website would like to buy them.

This is "travel writing" at its worst - banal diary entries of this and that of a twee class of traveler, not wealthy or privileged enough to feel guilty, not poor or deprived enough to be stuck, but that has just enough access to places and experiences to think how lucky I am to be able to witness this, let me share so others may vicariously revel in the wonder of this al fresco spa in Thailand.

It's writing as an aside, as a value-add to the writer's own experience, as if the writer is merely looking to fill the hours.

Even the phrase "middle-class housewife" makes me want to scratch myself frantically, if only because scratching myself till I bleed would be so much more interesting and exciting than having to listen to one more middle-class housewife drone on about her day at the "glorious spa resplendent with piles of fluffy white towels, gallons of Champagne and more hunky masseurs than you can ... *wink*." What? Lick a lip at? Suck caviar off? Wait, don't tell me. I have no idea what ladies who go on lunch-and-spa sessions would like to do to their masseurs and I'd like to keep it that way.

What we see less of and what we need more of these days is travel journalism, people in a new place deliberately seeking out stories of interest and of import, not merely content to waft through a five-day tour in air-conditioned jeeps and Michelin-starred restaurants and then write down their thoughts.

The observant among you may notice this chapter goes against the grain of what I've been advising so far - that you should be willing to do whatever your editor wants you to do. And many editors these days want exactly these kinds of articles, because that's exactly what the sales guys want, because that's exactly what the advertisers want. Consider this chapter a purist diversion where, for just a moment, we can imagine the travel-writing world as it ought to be.

And I'm not saying that all middle-classers cannot write or that luxurious experiences should be avoided - far from it. I use the character of an untroubled housewife/husband to illustrate a point - that quaint, precious, inoffensive prose has become standard in many if not most travel publications.

If you arrived on Earth from outer space and hoped to get a feel for what the world was like by reading in-flight magazines and many of the mainstream travel publications, you'd think it was one big smiley-faced celebration of happiness filled with Michelin-starred restaurants, sumptuous spas, acre upon acre of Asian paddy field, glistening swimming pools as big as meadows, people doing yoga on any available surface, pretty British villages, postcard beaches, screensaver temples and toned, tanned models - exactly the kind of world that appeals to empty-nesters with disposable income and time on their hands.

There are commercial reasons for this phenomenon. But anyone who actually travels knows that this represents a select niche in the experiences of travelers and that travel writing has a duty to report on the other stuff too.

So, if you're a housewife or a househusband (or write like one) and you want to make that lifestyle change, make it fully - verbally, tonally, ideologically. Don't just describe the spa as if that hasn't been done a thousand times already. Give me its stories, reveal its spirit, cut open its gut and let me see its organs, throbbing and pumping, spill out onto the polished floor with a visceral splat.

8 INSIDE CNN: FEEDING THE TROLLS, OR BEING ONE

I walk into the office with a tingle of anticipation running over my skin. My first written piece is going up today. It's November 2010, nine months after I join CNNGo, but the volume of content that's needed copyediting hasn't allowed for any writing, until now.

And I'm excited and nervous because the piece is a provocative op-ed titled "Drunken British expats should be chained up", an only partially tongue-in-cheek lament of some of the asinine behavior I've seen since moving into my apartment in Central, Hong Kong. It's part of a new series conceived by recently arrived executive editor Chuck Thompson called Tell Me About It … (Views, Opinion, Attitude) that squares neatly with our mission to be a kind of CNN in jeans, offering less formal, slightly more cavalier travel and lifestyle content.

It's a bit of an experiment, but Thompson himself is no stranger to controversial posts. And I'm encouraged by the reactions from both Zoe Li, who as Hong Kong editor is managing this post, and Thompson himself. Li is initially nervous of the topic, and could spike the piece entirely should she dislike what I file. But having read the piece she messages me on Skype: "I don't know how you can live copy editing our crap if you can write like this." And Thompson, when I tell him of her reaction and that it will be published, says: "Smart girl."

Editors down, it's now the reader reactions I focus on. I give it one final scan and hit publish. It doesn't occur to me how much these pieces have been designed so that CNN can distance itself from the opinions within, attaching them instead directly and solely to the writer. These pieces aren't just a headline with a small, italicized byline halfway down the page. Each piece has the writer's full name at the start of the headline. There's a full facial photograph at the top of the piece, accompanied with the writer's name again. There's a byline under the headline. And there's a disclaimer: The opinions voiced in this article are solely those of the author.

To this day, you can Google me and find these op-eds. They are an established, possibly un-deletable part of my online persona.

But like I say, that doesn't occur. In fact I enjoy the ownership of the piece, the soapbox feel, the attention. It's deliberately inflammatory and I'm not entirely sure what reactions to expect, or what to hope for. A few example lines:

"How many times do we have to hear about some beered-up banker arrested for indecently assaulting a taxi exhaust before we make an example of him?"

"Expats are the stray dogs of the working world. They arrive, they sniff around, and once they've eaten, humped or pissed on everything in sight, they move on."

"It's not the drinking that gets me, it's the drinking till you're so drunk you end up pouring that seventh shot of Sambuca in your eye rather than your mouth. Deliberately. Or the drinking till you're so drunk, you think that gorgeous Amazonian goddess with the cool shoulder tattoo at the bar just licked her lips at you, only to find out she's a he, the tattoo's a knife wound but sod it, you'll shag it anyway."

My greatest fear is that nothing happens. No Facebook likes, no comments, a few hundred pageviews and the empty silence of irrelevance.

I needn't have worried. Within an hour, the post receives a few dozen Facebook likes and several comments, above average in both regards at this point for CNNGo. The first comment is supportive, purporting to enjoy the humor in the piece. But then the invective starts. I'm an idiot, a non-journalist, a sad, pathetic waste of space with no life. How can CNN employ me? How can I call myself a travel writer or editor? I should go back to Britain, let the fun people carry on, stop being the party pooper, go kill myself.

The post is shared on other unaffiliated Facebook pages too. There, the irate outbursts are even less guarded, more abusive. Many, unsurprisingly, come from fellow Brits and I feel a small quiver of shame - that I've grassed up the home team. But I also feel vindicated.

And honestly, genuinely, the abuse doesn't affect me. It's my first real, personal insight into the world of the

Internet commenter and though I was a little surprised at the level of animosity directed at what is a perfectly true and verifiable observation (that many Brits act like hooligans after a few beers), the fact that people engaged is what counts.

The piece is just the first of several posts I write for the TMAI column over the next four years, all of which are deliberately contrarian, confrontational or challenging, designed to attract engagement, comments and shares. Their headlines include: "Why I hate museums", "Photography has ruined travel", "Evil spirits: The truth about Chinese New Year", "Why the 'white tax' is perfectly acceptable". I enjoy writing these pieces. They're cathartic and stimulating. The responses, good and bad, justify the time. But not all writers and editors are as casual about being abused by strangers.

While I write nine pieces under the TMAI banner, no other editor writes more than two. I see it as a fantastic opportunity to express a view, to experiment, to test and push boundaries, while others appear to see it as a good way to get slapped in the face.

I'm able to distance myself from the vilifying comments because I'm also able to distance myself from the articles. James Durston, the real-life human being, is quite different to James Durston the online opinion writer, whose goal is to inspire engagement and who chooses subjects and words most likely to achieve that.

Later one commenter gets close to catching on: "This author either really is an idiot or he's the best troll I've ever seen," he writes. That's another way of saying I'm an insincere writer, that I write for effect, for comments and for shares, rather than to disseminate the truth, at least my version of it. But I demur. These are my opinions. They're not fabrications of the intellect. They're just expressed in a way that has been proven to achieve their aims.

TALKING EDS

Chuck Thompson, author, travel writer and editor

Worst pitch?

Some favorite awful pitches I've seen over the years literally read like this: "Your publication/website is so shitty. Assign me a story and I'll make it better." Introducing yourself to a potential publishing partner with an insult might get your pitch passed around the office, but it generally won't get you an assignment.

Otherwise, aside from pitches littered with typos or addressed to a competing publication or website, my least favorite are pitches devoid of detail or examples.

If someone proposes a story on the 10 craziest theme hotels in the world but doesn't bother (or can't) name more than one crazy hotel in their pitch, you can be sure the story won't be any more enlightening.

How do I know? I've fallen for this pitch a couple times. Never again.

In general, you can assume any story will be about as interesting and well thought out as the pitch. Lazy pitch = lazy story.

Perfect pitch?

Sure, this creature exists.

It starts with a compelling headline that immediately conveys the essence of the story—"How to get the best deal on diamonds in India," "5 most scenic drives in the U.S. Midwest."

It includes a surprising stat or fact from a reliable

source—the average markup on diamonds in local markets is 2,000% according to the Indian Association of Tour Operators. It might include a great image or two attached, particularly if it's a story touting scenic wonder.

It's either written by or includes original interview quotes from a relevant expert or two—a master Indian diamond polisher or the author of a book on road trips across the United States.

It emphatically does not put the writer at the center of the story.

Assigns?
Other than fitting the tenor of whatever publication or website I'm assigning for, no common theme springs to mind. Ultimately it just has to be entertaining and there are endless ways to achieve that.

Writing goals?
To co-opt the advice of the Pet Shop Boys, the biggest sin of writing is being boring. I often try to keep readers entertained with humor. But you can entertain readers in lots of ways - with surprising facts, clever observations, strong opinions, "secret" information, compelling characters, dramatic events.

And always, always, always avoid clichés … like the plague.

--

Chuck Thompson is the author of five travel books and former executive producer of CNN Travel, editor in chief of *Travelocity* magazine and features editor for *Maxim*. www.chuckthompson.com

9 WHAT KIND OF PITCHER ARE YOU?

At regular points in your travel-writing career, it's useful to ask yourself: what kind of writer am I? Or better yet, what kind of writer do I want to be?

I spoke recently to a freelancer who already had a good profile and had established a wide network as a general freelancer for hire. She decided some months ago that she wanted to specialize in health writing, but had trouble drumming up interest without much experience or a specialist profile in the subject. Then, on a whim, she changed the title in her email signature and on her website from "Freelance writer" to "Health writer". Within days she was contacted by two potential clients interested in hiring her.

That's a story about branding, and how tiny adjustments in your approach and your communications can have impact. That's not quite what this chapter is about, but it speaks to the idea of carving a niche with which clients can readily identify you. And I don't just mean the usual news, features, golf/spa/cruise writing, destination specialisms etc, that are overpopulated already.

The list writer

The people I assigned most content to while at CNN were what I came to think of as 'list writers'. They didn't set out to become list writers, I'm sure, and I'm surer they don't have 'List writer' inscribed in their email signature. But through their willingness to do the lists I wanted, and to pitch them regularly, and, importantly, to provide all the add-ons such as pictures to go with each item in the list, they became my go-to sources for these types of article.

They weren't even very good writers, if truth be told, but they made up for that through their readiness to take on this work. And I published a lot of lists. Lists are the result of editors chasing pageviews. In fact, I consciously restricted these writers to lists, because I knew anything of greater depth, that required more journalism, would show their lack of skill and require much more work on my part to make right.

Lists don't need to be bullet paragraphs of a few dozen words, with pictures. I occasionally assign list pieces that involve several interviews, many hours of research, great writing and great editing … proper journalism, in other words, in list form. And that pays off. As per the formula described a few chapters back, the listicle headline would entice people into the story, and then the great content would inspire them to share it. And there could well be a niche to be carved here, if lists are to remain a high-traffic source regularly used by editors, of listicle content that is also high quality.

Editors love lists because not only does the format appeal to readers, but they're ready-made for galleries or slideshows of pictures, which can earn even more pageviews. The tech guys that built our site enabled a feature where every click of a slideshow would add to the pageview count without refreshing the page. For an extended period slideshow posts made up nearly every piece of content I published, for exactly this reason.

But many writers still sneer at lists, and unless you have a week free to produce something of higher quality (this type of post, by its nature, may require more than the average amount of research time) the lure of the quickie Googled list of ten items, 80 words each and a few PR-sourced pics is hard to resist. In fact, I see a lot of evidence to suggest this is what most readers want too. Read the comment sections of especially non-moderated content sites, and you'll note that many readers appear not to be readers at all, but rather scanners, merely glancing at the list item headings to see if the list is in fact the Top 10 Movies About Water Ever Made, and if not, gushing forth with their own list, after furiously chastising the writer, editor and entire publishing company involved for making such a terrible article. The point is they still clicked, and commented, and possibly shared, and as long as the almighty page view count keeps climbing, we editors will keep assigning.

Visitors want quick, bite-sized snacks when they click into a list - the Internet is a buffet don't forget - and quickie

Googled lists may hit that demand more efficiently, and cost-effectively, than fully researched lists with added journalism. At CNN we always said, sometimes at the top of list articles, "these lists are meant to start conversations, not end them."

I used two writers most regularly. Writer A eventually was blacklisted for plagiarizing PR copy from websites (more on that in chapter 14). But before that she wrote 32 articles for me in 18 months, for US$9,325.

Writer B wrote 25 pieces in 14 months for US$8,400.

So you don't need to be great to make a living in this trade - you just need to do the dirty work no one else wants to.

Those of you good with arithmetic will note the average cost per article was around US$310. Not a huge amount for roughly 1,000 words of copy as well as sourcing around ten images for each post. But that's not too shabby as far as online pay rates go, especially for a list - once you know what's required you should be able to bash out this kind of piece in a day.

The writer-photographer duo

Another writer I always enjoyed using, and would have used more had she pitched more, was one who deliberately, rather than by accident as above, set herself and her husband up as a team that could provide text and great pictures as a package. Reporters and editors face a daily frustration: getting good photography for posts. And if someone comes along who says they can provide great photography, on an exclusive basis and within the fee you offer, you're going to bite. In fact, you might even raise your fee a little above the standard rate, as I did.

The pro

You'd be surprised how many bad writers make it into this profession. This is even more apparent in non-English-speaking markets, where competition is low.*

You've already seen some of the bad pitches I had to deal with on a regular basis. So it's actually not that hard to establish yourself in the eyes of an editor, particularly one in a non-English-speaking land, as a proper pro, someone who takes their job seriously and who will be easy to work with. All you have to do is be that proper pro. Write good pitches. Hit your deadlines. Respond quickly and collaboratively. Submit clean copy. Do your fact checking. Aspire to excellence.

It's easy for jobbing journos to pressurize themselves into churnalism. The need simply to be published, to get that paycheck, and the relief you feel whenever someone gives you a job, can mean you rarely scrutinize the quality of the work you do. You pump those stories out, taking on as many assignments as are offered, conscious there may be a slow period around the corner.

--

*Incidentally, if I were to give one tip to wannabe writers wondering what they can do to make themselves stand out a little from the crowd, it would be: move to a country where there's a demand for English writing, but where English writers are sparse. The United States, It pays to step back occasionally and define what it is you really want to do, and how you want to be perceived as a writer.

Canada, the UK, Australasia, even South Africa, to some extent, have highly competitive English writing and journalism trades. The greatest thing a university leaver could do is leave these English-speaking cauldrons and live somewhere their natural skillset will instantly set them above the average.

10 INSIDE CNN: CNNGO
BREAKS THROUGH

"Won an iPhone, lost an iPhone, turbans and
hard hats, an $800 round, a police station and
some puking. Solid Friday night."

My Facebook status update after the Turner Broadcasting
Spring Dinner of 2011 (Turner being the parent company
of CNN) sheds no light on the context of the events that
occur the previous night. But for me, and no doubt others
in the team, it's a breakthrough of sorts, a signal that
CNNGo is metamorphosing from an experimental blog
into a legitimate travel website that CNN is happy to
encourage and even accept as an extension of what it does.

It's 15 months after I join and all appears to be going
great. While we're still modeled on a "blog," for want of a
better term, operating on the CNN sidelines, while we're
all hustling on a daily basis, pumping out a large volume of

disparate, disconnected content and don't have time to consider what's happening around and above us, our traffic stats are going up month after month without a single exception and we can see we're at least gaining an audience. At the same time we've been gearing up for the launch of our seventh and eighth cities, Sydney and Seoul - the first expansion of the site since it was launched 18 months previously - and plans are in place for four Asian language sites too.

We're still stuck on the 30th floor in the building with empty desks for neighbors (the CNN newsroom proper is up on the 40th), but the mood for the most part is buoyant.

The only sign, for those with the 360 vision to notice, that the wider CNN brotherhood may not consider us the superstars we think we are is the lack of direct, attributable, positive feedback from an unaffiliated exec. Andrew Demaria and Chuck Thompson readily pat our backs at the end of each month with a group phone call celebrating "another record traffic month" and Thompson especially is good at firing out emails not just to condemn shoddy stories but also to praise the great. But that feels a little like your mom proclaiming your fantastic refrigerator artwork. The real sign of wider recognition from within CNN is still absent.

But then, during the Turner Spring Dinner of March 2011, an event as big in this part of the world as Christmas or Thanksgiving is in the West, it arrives.

The ballroom of the five-star hotel is subtly lit in reds and blues. Large, round dining tables scatter the floor. A stage with a huge TV screen forms the focal point. The entire CNNGo team is present, with editors having flown in from Mumbai, Singapore, Bangkok, Tokyo and Shanghai. Other Turner departments are here too: Cartoon Network, TCM, Warner Bros TV and more. The fancy dress theme is Icons of 2011; we've donned bright yellow hardhats as homage to the Chilean miners who had been stuck for weeks underground, were rescued and became massive global media darlings. I've had several glasses of wine already, as have many others, and the event is yet to formally begin.

As we're ushered to our seats and the wine glasses are refilled, Steve Marcopoto, president and managing director of Turner International in APAC, takes the stage. I can't recall anything of his speech except this: that he mentions Andrew Demaria and CNNGo by name at least twice in his address.

And that's the moment. This is when I feel some relief that the traffic drives, the volume of content, the work, sweat and effort is actually getting noticed beyond the thin grey walls of our office. For Demaria, the face of our brand, to be mentioned personally is telling. These kinds of things may seem inconsequential for anyone not au fait with the over-sensitized politics of a large corporate office network. But that decision to name Demaria and our brand would not have been taken lightly. It means we're on track. We can be revealed to the wider company. It means Marcopoto is probably also talking about us to his peers and seniors back in Atlanta. Even if we're not yet profitable.

It's no coincidence it's our team that virtually sprints onto the dance floor once the speeches and dinner are over and tears it up, not exactly Wolf of Wall Street style blowing through heaps of cocaine, hookers, cocktails and supercars, but like people who feel valued, shaking our butts like champions in a room full of much more experienced, senior and successful media personalities. We are CNNGo, we flaunt. We're doing things traditional, conservative CNN hasn't tried before. We feel like people who are good at their jobs, and we feel valued.

That confidence follows us into Lan Kwai Fong as we determine the end of the Spring Dinner should not mean the end of the night, and it's here that things get messy. Sambuca shots are ordered, by me, which come to $800. Having won an iPhone 4 earlier in the night during the traditional raffle that goes with all Spring Dinners, and given it to Hong Kong editor Zoe Li to look after as I have no bag, she reveals she's lost her bag, or, more likely, someone has stolen it. At the police station, while reporting the loss/theft, another young female staffer provides her contribution to my later Facebook post, the vomiting.

I do make it back to my apartment this time without sending abusive texts to the boss or getting distracted by an overpriced club, but I wouldn't know it from the head pains the next day.

11 FEES: WHY I DON'T PAY MORE (BUT SOMETIMES DO)

All writers would love to earn a dollar a word. I've written in the past that if publishers aren't going to raise their rates for decades in some cases, or continue to pay lowly fees, then freelancers should be able to resell articles verbatim to other publishers until they DO earn a dollar a word.

That is possibly wishful thinking on my part, though I do seriously suggest you at least ask your next client for a contract that doesn't hand over all rights into perpetuity to them. I was urged at CNN to get contributors to sign an agreement that gave CNN universal rights to the content on acceptance. We did however have a second, more generous contract available for photographers, which gave rights to CNN for six months and then allowed for shared rights between CNN and the photographer. Not perfect, but the photographer could then at least resell those photos elsewhere and earn more money from them.

Why photographers? Because they always kicked up the biggest fuss about rights. They asked for a better deal. It was a mini battle that they won, simply by fighting it. I see no reason why writers shouldn't try the same.

Until then though we are stuck with the legacy contracts that tend to mean once an article is sold, it's dead to you. At least in terms of its cash-generating ability.

But believe it or not, all editors would love to be able to pay a dollar a word too. And, sometimes, while they might not be able to pay this dreamy amount, they can often dig into their budgetary pockets a little deeper and fork out a little more. But they won't if you don't ask.

If you do want to squeeze a little more cash out of your existing clients, it may help to have a little insight into how editorial budgets work.

Haggling over fees is a tiresome, sometimes daily exercise. Fee debates I think cause more editor headaches than anything else (besides comment box trolls). But I don't for a second suggest freelancers just suck it up and be grateful they're getting paid anything (I believe the contrary). Sometimes I simply cannot pay more, and having to apologize weekly for having no budget and for disappointing writers and sometimes losing great features as a result, is painful. I know why writers are always asking to be paid more, especially regular writers whom the editor clearly enjoys working with. And I know the fees I paid (at CNN at least) were low to middling at best. I always wished I could pay more. I just really couldn't.

But some of the time I could.

Different publications work in different ways, but in every magazine or website I've worked at I would be given a monthly budget along with a quota of content pieces to publish within that month/budget. That's fairly standard. A smart editor will always try and get a slightly bigger budget than he really needs (and his manager/editor will do the same thing one step further up the chain). When asked to come up with a budget that would help get the kind of content, and the kind of traffic, we needed when we turned from CNNGo into CNN Travel, I asked for US$12,000 a month. I was given around US$4,500. That was my budget, to be used for homepage content. That fluctuated a little each year when new budgets were decided, but over the four years I assigned stories at CNN (February 2011 to August 2014) I spent about US$165,000 on freelancers. We also had eight city editors, later stripped down to an Asia editor, a Europe editor (also covering EMEA) and a North/South America editor (also covering the Caribbean), each of whom had their own budgets, a little less than mine. Some months I didn't even use my entire budget. And that meant when good writers asked nicely for a little extra, and justified it by offering something extra themselves, or argued well that the piece and the work they needed to do warranted it, I would often give it. Often it was a small lift - say from US$300 to US$350 - but having been a freelancer I know this is appreciated and helps with the grocery shopping. The point is - ask.

And ask nicely. Entitled demands for higher fees because you get paid a dollar a word at T&L may get you a higher fee, this time. But you'll also put me in a negative frame of mind, which makes it easier for me to silently hate you, which makes it easier for me to say no next time.

It helps too to have established yourself in my mind as a pro. Or to have established yourself as a writer who offers something different or special and of a high quality. Good freelance writers are frustratingly thin on the ground (especially outside of the main English-speaking countries), so if you are a good writer there's a niche there that can be filled without too much hard work. I think the average fee I paid writers was around US$300 per 1,000-word story, and that was above average even within CNN Travel. That's not enough to interest the very best writers, meaning there's an opportunity there for the right-minded people and/or newcomers.

CNN paid these fees because it knew it would still be able to interest writers due to its reach and brand name. As one of the best-distributed media platforms in the world the exposure you can get through a platform like CNN is immense. But click around any writer's forum, and "exposure" would seem to be a dirty word. "Exposure doesn't pay my mortgage" is a common argument against accepting high distribution in lieu of hard cash. "Exposure kills people" is another. And that's true. I've always believed that if an editor and a publication think your article is good enough to run, they should also think it's good enough to buy. Don't be entitled or greedy, but don't be a martyr either.

Many places don't like to accept articles for free as part of a legal position. I was warned away from accepting freebies, to the point of offering a token amount of money such as US$25, just so CNN could then legally claim to own the article and do with it what it wanted. The only writer who refused to accept my money was an investment banker who just had a good story he wanted to tell. Our lowly fee simply wasn't worth the trouble of an invoice. Other editors will beg you to accept a low or zero-sum fee. Those at HuffPo spring to mind. And many freelancer bloggers these days instruct not to back up. Stand your ground. Demand to be rewarded for the hard yards you put in.

I used to think there are two exceptions to this: 1) You're brand new and need to build a portfolio. 2) You're not very good (i.e. have an inferior product to sell).

But I've since changed my mind and now would never tell any writer trying to write professionally to give anything away for free. And I include social platforms such as LinkedIn and Medium. It's too easy today to create your own blog and use that as a portfolio if you want a place to show off your writing to a potential client.

Something else to bear in mind is that most if not all magazines and websites do not have a single set fee. Editors have their beats, and each beat has a monthly budget, and each editor has the freedom to use that budget as they want (within reason) to hit their goals. Which means different writers get paid different amounts, depending on numerous criteria: quality, professionalism, new writer versus established, the country they live in, whether they provide any "extras" (such as photography) and so on. That said, editors must stick to a rough guideline. My fees tended to fluctuate between US$250 and US$350 on average, with more paid for bigger or more complex pieces. At the publication I joined after CNN, fees vary wildly, from around ten US cents per word for a web piece written by a Chinese writer, to nearly US$2 per word for a magazine piece from a well-regarded British personality.

12 INSIDE CNN: MONSTERS

In August 2014 CNN disables comments on all online articles. The editor can activate them again manually if he or she wants, but is advised to do so only on articles that "have the potential for high-quality debate -- and when writers and editors can actively participate in and moderate those conversations."

Around the same time several other high profile websites including Reuters, Popular Science and the Chicago Sun-Times do the same, or scale back their comment sections. And later others too: Bloomberg, The Verge, The Daily Beast, Motherboard.

Comments have become a staple of the online experience and are actively encouraged by many publishers so they can measure engagement on content and then use that as part of their ad sell strategy. The reason for turning them off shouldn't surprise anyone. Trolls.

The rise of the troll has a pernicious effect on the

Internet. CNN, with its huge international reach, is a favorite troll target giving them what they want in abundance: distribution, attention and interaction. CNN's community manager sends a memo around just before comments are disabled, lamenting the "the abusive, vulgar and mean-spirited trolling that plagues a lot of our stories."

But while they're annoying, not all trolls are like that. Sometimes they're funny. One regular commenter on CNN Travel is a guy whose handle is Troll Trollson. That's pretty funny. And his comments aren't mean-spirited or abusive, just provocative. Another posts dozens of comments most weeks, absolutely unrelated to the articles above them, detailing the fictional love lives of a rabbit and a hedgehog. Many others though, particularly out of the United States, use any article as an opportunity to make politically or racially or socially pointed remarks. It's these the CNN community guys want to avoid when they decide to turn comments off.

I'm disappointed. One of the great things about working online is seeing the instant feedback from your audience. But I understand it as well. Ultimately trolls degrade the brand, putting an unfortunate section of the readership on display for potential advertisers to see.

And we shouldn't think that trolls operate only in the public spaces of article comment boxes.

We all have a little troll inside us, and if we're not careful and don't keep it well contained it can escape onto the pages of a social media platform or an email. I regularly meet writers - scarred, possibly psychopathic, entitled, disgruntled types - who let their inner troll break out.

I only have email contact with these shining examples of how not to be, but despite this limited access to their true psyche I quickly understand them to be three-beer monsters.

I'm sure you know the type. You go to the bar for an introductory meeting, and through beer one they're charming, funny, friendly and smiley and you start thinking you've found not just a writer to work with but a guy to have a drink with and maybe even spend an occasional afternoon watching a sporting event with too.

Beer two comes, and as he progresses toward the bottom of the glass he starts to voice controversial or strange views, the charm has worn down to a thin veneer coating an angry inner world, and you decide ok, just a writer then.

Halfway through beer three he's turned a startling shade of pink, spittle whips out of his mouth every second sentence and as well as calling you names, abusing your professionalism and complaining loudly about the meager size of your fees, he's all about ready to smash a bottle over the waiter's head simply for being close to hand.

Stress is a common feature of the writing and editing world. As is inebriation. Anyone who says they find writing easy probably isn't doing it right. But part of being a pro is not giving in to the urge to blast off that incendiary comment, however unrecognized your talent may be.

Japan is a hotbed for moderately insane expat writers. The place either attracts them or they go mad while there. Either way, editors often have to deal with the effects. One Tokyo-based writer, whom I don't deal with myself for features, toward the end of his relationship with us (in fact, his final email is the nail in the coffin) writes to the two senior editors on staff, Andrew Demaria and Chuck

Thompson, and copies myself. It lands during the wee hours, 3 or 4 am, and the whole message reeks of late night karaoke and sake. He recklessly abuses Demaria and Thompson and wishes me luck dealing with these two "incompetents". It's hilarious in not just its obnoxiousness but also its fallaciousness. I have no idea why he has written the email (there's nothing in it to imply a reason) and I instantly Google the writer to see what he's written for us and what else he has online. I find two mediocre features he has done for CNN Travel and, among other things, a picture of him on his blog looking overweight and pallid, a sun-averse Brit cavorting in a sumo belt. Needless to say he's blacklisted and informed so with an admirably restrained email from Thompson.

Another young Japan-based expat writer expresses his pitch in the form of a haiku. I write back:

"Haiku pitch comes in
Editor regrets to say
This is not for me"

Another Japan contributor who has the very correct impression that we're ignoring him makes repeated attempts via email to find out why we're no longer friends. Later he calls the offices and is put through to one of our junior editor, who spends a few minutes fumbling her way shyly through his interrogation before I take the call myself and tell him directly, "You've obviously done something to upset the senior managers here, I don't know what that is but I'm afraid we're on instruction not to use you again and that's got to be the end of it."

There's a pause, and a sniff, and then: "Well, I don't need you guys you know. I don't NEED you. But I like what you do and this is a conspiracy. This is a total conspiracy."

To be fair his dealings with me were always reasonable, but when I do a little research on him and uncover tales of defamation, lying, how he's been harassed by officials, deported and threatened, I'm glad not to hear from him again.

But not all the world's crazy freelancers live in Japan. One writer, with whom I get along well until the final email string, was a fellow Brit. I know instantly there's something a little off. Unusually for a writer, he sends in fully written, completed features cold. The first time he writes he sends about a dozen. Sending full features in cold is not always a bad thing, but if you do that your feature has to be perfect. Anything I see in a supposedly finished piece that doesn't look right is another reason for me to say no. His pieces are strewn with errors and idiosyncrasies that were it not for an impressive wit, would have seen me reaching for the delete button. His punctuation is like a random exercise of flinging commas and periods haphazardly through his paragraphs rather than an intuitive process abiding by the laws of grammar. And his choice of font is bemusing - I can't recall exactly which it was, but it was thick, black and barely legible. **Something like this**. Imagine a full 1,000-word feature written in that. Again, not a deal breaker, as it's easy enough to change a font in Word for editing. But one of several signs that should have warned me this guy has circles where he needed squares.

Had he not been on some interesting escapades (a visit to the self-proclaimed "world's ugliest town", a visit to the Tokyo earthquake simulator) and were he not in fact a very entertaining writer (some of his lines were among the funniest we published) he would have been instantly discarded. But publish him we did, and I'm pleased when Chuck agrees with me that his first piece is certainly idiosyncratic, but perhaps, possibly, genius too.

I use him for at least a year and my replacement continues to use him after I leave CNN. But in my final month, the semblance of a professional manner deserts him when I tell him I'm changing jobs and I wouldn't be able to use him at my new venture (a luxury wine magazine). He takes it as a veiled attack on the quality of his work, and there follows a series of around 20 emails, all one or two lines, that feel to me like a boiling over - he had held it together well enough for a year, but suddenly the valve has broken and he's erupting.

There's swearing, there are references to previously held publications ("Don't you know I used to write for XXX?!"), there are bizarre non-sequiturs in a style I learn to associate uniquely with him. I'm aware that had we been face to face in an office or even in a bar (I don't think he's a three-beer monster), he likely wouldn't boil over quite so energetically. It's much easier to be rude and obnoxious when you're sitting at home behind your own desk, firing emails to someone who's thousands of miles away and whom you've never met. The comments section trolls are testament to that.

But you still need to be lacking in what most of us would consider fairly standard tantrum controls to send emails like these.

*

TALKING EDS

Phoebe Smith, travel writer, author and editor of Wanderlust travel magazine

Worst pitch?
I received a pitch for a golfing feature in Dubai. We never cover golf and Dubai is not a very Wanderlust-y destination. I'd have looked if they had surprised me with a unique reason we should cover Dubai, but golf? Straight in the bin. And they didn't know who to pitch to.

Perfect pitch?
Yes. I get them regularly from good freelancers. They include an article idea that's perfect for my readers, new, fresh, and tells me immediately where it will fit into my magazine. They know my readers, they know what my readers want (which is - incidentally - exactly what I want). They keep it brief and too the point without filling it full of fluffy PR-speak.

Assigns?
They are completely right for my readers - they will excite them, inspire them and, occasionally, surprise them. My readers are the most important people in the world to me - without them I have no magazine.

Writing goals?
Exactly the same. Whoever I am writing for it will be aimed at their readers. It's not about what I want and what

I enjoy, I am merely the person that takes them to a place through my words and I am as harsh with myself as I would be with anyone. It's not enough that I want to go there it's why the reader would want to go there. That is always key.

--

Phoebe Smith is author of seven books on adventure and the outdoors including Extreme Sleeps: Adventures of a Wild Camper, Wild Nights: Camping Britain's Extremes and Wilderness Weekends: Wild Adventures in Britain's Rugged Corners. www.phoebe-smith.com

13 85 PLACES TO PITCH
AND WHAT THEY PAY

Here's a selection of publications, print and online, travel writers should know about. This list is far from exhaustive, but it's a good starting point for creating your own go-to list of platforms that offer freelance travel writing work and are worth pitching.

I've included links to the contact forms or writer guidelines where I could find them, though wasn't possible in every case.

This list mostly consists of publications that publish international stories from various locations, to cater to your globetrotting escapades.

And I've only included publications that pay, even if some of them pay very little. No fee = no-no.

Unless the guidelines state otherwise, it's always best to

write directly to the editor of the section your idea fits best, with most names and email addresses easily found these days with a bit of Googling or searching on LinkedIn.

Decent fees (US$0.65+ per word):

AFAR: http://about.afar.com/about/guidelines-and-terms/writers-guidelines/

Arrive (Amtrak): http://amtrakmedianetwork.com/print

Backpacker: http://www.backpacker.com/backpacker-contributor-s-guidelines/

Better Homes and Gardens: http://www.bhg.com/bhg/file.jsp?item=/help/writersGuidelines

Coastal Living: http://www.coastalliving.com/contact-us

Condé Nast Traveller: http://www.cntraveller.com/contact-us

Contract: http://www.contractdesign.com/contact.shtml

Departures: http://www.departures.com/contact-us

Eating Well: http://www.eatingwell.com/writers_guidelines

Family Circle: http://www.familycircle.com/writers-guidelines-1/

LA Times Travel: http://www.latimes.com/la-trw-guidelines-story-story.html

LE PAN: http://www.lepanmedia.com/about/

National Geographic Traveler:
http://travel.nationalgeographic.com/travel/traveler-magazine/about-us/writer-guidelines/

New York Magazine: http://nymag.com/contactus/

Outside Magazine:
http://www.outsideonline.com/contact-us

The Sun Magazine:
http://thesunmagazine.org/about/submission_guidelines/writing

The Wayfarer (from AFAR):
http://about.afar.com/about/guidelines-and-terms/writers-guidelines-the-wayfarer/

Travel + Leisure:
http://www.travelandleisure.com/contact#ed

Middling fees (US$0.30-0.65 per word):

Alaska Airlines Magazine:
http://www.alaskaairlinesmagazine.com/contributor/guidelines/

BBC Travel:
http://www.bbc.com/travel/story/20160106-bbc-travel-author-brief

Canadian Geographic:
http://www.canadiangeographic.ca/careers

CNN Travel: http://travel.cnn.com/about/

Cruising World: http://www.cruisingworld.com/cruising-world-guidelines-writers-and-photographers

Delta Sky: http://www.deltaskymag.com/About-Delta-Sky/Writers-Guidelines.aspx

Earth: http://www.earthmagazine.org/for-authors

Four Seasons Magazine:
http://www.fourseasons.com/magazine/contact

Hana Hou! (Hawaiian Airlines):
http://www.hanahou.com/pages/about.asp?PageID=2#WritersGuidelines

High Life (British Airways):
http://highlife.ba.com/contact/

Independent:
http://www.independent.co.uk/service/external-contributors-policy-7905982.html

Motorhome: http://www.motorhome.com/wp-content/uploads/2011/12/WritersGuidelines.pdf

Open Skies (Emirates):
http://www.openskiesmagazine.com/

Small Boats Monthly:
http://smallboatsmonthly.com/editorial-guidelines/

The Atlantic: http://www.theatlantic.com/faq/#37

The Guardian:
https://www.theguardian.com/info/1999/nov/22/contributors-guide-and-contacts

The New York Times:
http://www.nytimes.com/ref/travel/SUBMISSION.html

The Times/The Sunday Times:
https://login.thetimes.co.uk/links/contact

Tiger Tales (Tigerair): http://ink-live.com/emagazines/tiger-tales-asia

USA Today: http://www.usatoday.com/travel/

Wanderlust:
http://www.wanderlust.co.uk/aboutus/writers

Washington Post: http://www.washingtonpost.com/wp-dyn/content/article/2005/10/31/AR2005103100911.html

Low fees (less than US$0.30 per word):

Alpinist: http://www.alpinist.com/p/magazine/contribute

Atlas Obscura: http://www.atlasobscura.com/work-with-us#freelance

BootsnAll: http://www.bootsnall.com/writers/bootsnall-feature-articles.shtml

Broken Jaw Travel:
http://www.brokenjawtravel.com/submissions

Buzzfeed:
https://www.buzzfeed.com/rachelysanders/how-to-pitch-buzzfeed-life

Eastern Fly Fishing:

http://www.matchthehatch.com/EasternFlyFishing/Writers Guidelines

Edible Communities:
http://www.ediblecommunities.com/content/index.php?option=com_contact&view=contact&id=1&Itemid=200075

GoNOMAD: http://www.gonomad.com/travel-writer-guidelines

Island: http://islandmag.com/pages/submit

Matador:
http://matadornetwork.com/content/contributors-and-job-applicants/

Oregon Coast:
http://www.oregoncoastmagazine.com/guidlin.php

Pathfinders Travel: http://pathfinderstravel.com/wp-content/uploads/2014/08/WRITERS-GUIDELINES1.pdf

Perceptive Travel:
http://www.perceptivetravel.com/guidelines.html

SouthWest Fly Fishing:
http://www.matchthehatch.com/SouthwestFlyFishing/Writers Guidelines

Unknown fees (but worth pitching):

Africa Geographic:
http://africageographic.com/magazine-contributions/

American Way (American Airlines): http://www.ink-live.com/emagazines/american-way

Atlanta Jounal-Constitution: http://www.myajc.com/staff/

Cruise Travel: http://www.cruisetravelmag.com/ctravel_contact.php

DestinAsian: http://www.destinasian.com/contribute/

Dreamscapes: http://www.dreamscapes.ca/contact_us.php

Hemispheres/Rhapsody (United Airlines): http://www.unitedmags.com/

Fah Thai (Bangkok Airways): http://www.ink-live.com/emagazines/fah-thai?page=1

Going Places (Malaysia Airlines): http://www.goingplacesmagazine.com/website/editorial

International Traveller: http://www.internationaltravellermag.com/about-us/

Islands: http://www.islands.com/contact-us

Lonely Planet: http://www.lonelyplanet.com/careers/#become-a-contributor

Matter (Medium): https://medium.com/@lotto/would-you-like-to-pitch-medium-s-in-house-publications-matter-and-backchannel-27cb772e6705#.qrr8pbb4e

Metropolitan: http://www.eurostar.com/uk-en/travel-info/your-trip/metropolitan-magazine

Orbitz: https://www.orbitz.com/blog/

Outpost Magazine:
http://www.outpostmagazine.com/25-outpost-
information/173-contributor-guidelines-contribute-to-our-
travel-magazine-and-travel-website

Pacific Yachting: http://www.pacificyachting.com/writer-
submission-guidelines

Sunset: http://www.sunset.com/general/travel-writers

The Wayward Post:
http://thewaywardpost.com/contribute

Transitions Abroad:
http://www.transitionsabroad.com/information/writers/
writers.shtml

Travel Africa: http://travelafricamag.com/contribute/

Westjet Magazine:
http://www.westjetmagazine.com/write-us

Wonderland:
http://www.wonderlandmagazine.com/contact/

Yachting: http://www.yachtingmagazine.com/contact-us

A regularly updated version of this list can be found at:
http://travelwriteearn.com/publications-offer-freelance-
travel-writing-jobs/

14 INSIDE CNN: WHEN IT
ALL GOES WRONG

CNN Travel is not what one would call a hard-hitting news or investigative site. But occasionally posts are published that reverberate around the entire organization, due to the impact they have on readers.

Some of these are my own provocative opinion pieces. But while these elicit complaints, guffaws and other satisfying-to-slightly-alarming reactions thanks to social media and the comments box, it's not until I publish another piece, written by an intern, that I really get an insight into quite how deep the CNN brand can cut.

The sinful cities calamity

It's April 2011, and we've started taking on interns from Hong Kong University's Master of Journalism course. For the most part our intern intake is more hassle than it's worth. For some, English is an imperfect second language. For others, the standards required of an international media organization appear hard to grasp. For nearly all, the requirements of the work in practice are a world apart from the theory they're taught in the lecture halls of J-school.

Some interns do well however, and one of those is Andrew Willis, a bright, fastidious, slightly anxious young guy with a pallid complexion and a head of pale honey-colored hair. When he's told to move from the far side of the office to be closer to the team, he nervously asks me later if it's because our editor had seen him checking Facebook the previous day, and wanted to keep eyes on him. Of course it's nothing of the sort, and thusly naive about the workings of a modern digital media enterprise, Willis sets about uploading content, hunting down images and doing other grunt work the rest of the team can't face.

My policy is always to get interns to write at least a few short reblogs and couple of features while they're with us. My reasoning is that it helps get some of the easier content done and published while also giving interns a little reward and incentive for keeping on with the other daily tiresome and thankless tasks. Chuck Thompson is less generous, saying if an intern doesn't earn and deserve a shot at a byline, they shouldn't be given one out of charity. I can see his point. A badly written post from an intern would often take twice as long to fix up as writing the thing myself in the first place. But I generally ignore his advice on this particular topic, and so Willis started writing pieces too.

One day he pitches an idea along the lines of "Taipei top for street food lovers" based on a news post he's seen. I smell an opportunity to boost what would be a simple news post into something bigger, and suggest he angles it "How to get fat in Taipei". A couple more minutes of thought later, and the angle becomes "Asia's most sinful cities", declaring one city in Asia as the best (or worst) for each of the seven sins, starting with gluttony for Taipei.

To cut to the chase, we publish the piece not knowing or really worrying about how it would be received, and for a few hours nothing much happens. It's only the next day, when a mainstream Taiwanese newspaper has seen our post and reproduced parts of it themselves, that the comment flood starts, with hostile Taiwanese posting in their hundreds to defend what they see as a slight by a Western media titan, an American media titan no less, on their culinary honor.

That weekend I receive an exasperated phone call from Willis, who appears to be genuinely fearful after receiving death threats in his personal email account. I attempt to placate him, assuring him I've seen this sort of thing before and he needn't be concerned, but it has little effect. He even threatens to sue CNN.

It then becomes a political episode when Andrew Demaria goes to meet with and offer an apology to one of Taiwan's diplomatic officials in Hong Kong. The fact the post was complimenting Taipei's culinary scene seems to be disregarded.

As usual with these things it soon dies down, the irate Internet commenters find another target to attack and we move on to the next story. Willis speaks to me later and apologizes for the phone call and "for being such a newbie".

The revolting foods fiasco

Chinese readers are at us just two months later.

One of CNN's proud successes is CNN iReport, a system for getting free content from readers onto the site. We put up an iReport assignment titled "Your most revolting food experience". Among those submitted are fried tarantulas, fried frog, stir-fried cicadas and - the one that sets it all alight - century eggs, a Chinese dish of eggs pickled in ginger, turning them black and somewhat rotten-looking and enhancing the eggy taste. Danny Holwerda, the contributor of this dish, writes: "It's awful - - it tastes like the devil cooked eggs for me. It tastes like something that used to be an egg, but made some really horrible choices."

That's enough to set the Chinese netizenry off on a comment-athon against American food, CNN and America in general. Once again the writer receives numerous death threats in his personal email account. China's biggest food manufacturer throws their eggs in the ring demanding an apology and CNN duly relents. Andrew Demaria posts a lengthy apology explaining how the post was created and that the views of the iReporters in no way represent the views of CNN.

"Let us be very clear. This article was not meant to offend in any way anyone who likes century eggs, anyone who dislikes century eggs, any century egg manufacturers, anyone who works in the manufacturing or serving of century egg and especially Chinese culture."

Everything then dies down, and people appear to forget it ever happened.

The ugly monuments misunderstanding

We learn our lessons and manage not to piss anyone

off to this extent for about 18 months.

Then, in January 2014, we publish "The world's ugliest monuments."

As if a pressure-cooker filled with shit has been on the boil for the last year and a half, when this thing blows, it blows big. It doesn't just hit the fan, it destroys it into twisted, buckled fragments. The mess spreads across continents. It isn't something a quick online apology can clear up.

You can probably guess by now what happened. We publish a list of what we decide to call "The world's ugliest monuments" and one group is particularly upset by the inclusion of something they hold dear. This time it's Belarus and Russia, upset that the Courage Monument in Brest, commemorating Russian soldiers who died defending Brest Fortress from the Nazis in World War II, has been described as looking "either very angry or just constipated."

Politicians from Russia and Belarus condemned the "blasphemous" article, a U.S. diplomat is summoned to the Belarusian Foreign Ministry to explain the matter, CNN is forced to apologize and then, in a sign of how seriously this is being taken, removes the entire article from the site, with the apology note in its place. None of the other posts mentioned in this chapter is removed.

This is a particularly embarrassing episode for our editors, given that we had by now become an established part of the main CNN brand, with our own navigation tab on the website, marketing time and money spent, sales opportunities explored and senior executive eyes spending at least a little time on us. As CNNGo, this would have almost been expected, given that we were an experimental blog high on irreverence and voice. As CNN Travel, this is a serious international and diplomatic incident that threatens to at least taint, if not seriously damage, the brand values and business opportunities we've worked so hard to establish.

Throughout CNNGo and CNN Travel's lives, despite the traffic growth every month, targets being beaten and successes at every turn, we're constantly under pressure to justify our existence. Events like this undermine this mission, and it's no surprise that the very next month the editor who commissioned the piece (and who declined to comment on the incident when I contacted him) is fired. (In truth, his relationship to the senior eds is always a little rocky and it's unlikely this single incident leads to his dismissal. But it's certainly the final blow to the final nail in the coffin)

The hotel sex shambles

Scroll forward nine months during which we again manage not to offend anyone too badly, and we arrive at a piece of content that I suspect comes close to getting me fired too.

A blogger cold-mails me with an idea that I like - her personal take on the advantages of living in hotels for 200-300 days of the year, as she does with her traveling businessman husband.

Her piece includes items such as perfect sleep, dignified breakfasts, peaceful lobbies and, the item that causes the fiasco, wild sex. I immediately see my chance to get the click-grab headline I usually seek, move the wild sex item into the first spot on the list from the fifth and publish it with the headline "Why sex is better in hotels - and other confessions of a constant traveler."

I anticipate some kind of reaction from readers, in the form of lots of clicks and comments. I even dare to hope the comments would agree and appreciate the candid and somewhat humorous nature of the piece.

So the incendiary attack that plays out in the form of hundreds of venomous comments surprises me. I would say it even shocks me, and I don't get shocked easily. The writer's called all manner of obnoxious names ("Slut!" "Whore!" "Hack!"), her character's slurred, her behavior and relationship called into question. It is, in my view, a disgusting display of cowardly, self-righteous bullying from behind the safe wall of the anonymous comment box.

Within a few hours I receive an impressively calm email from the writer, bemoaning the nature of Internet commenters. A few hours after that I get another from her, slightly more fraught, saying this thing has blown out of all proportion, her bosses have found out and have fired her. I can't say if that's true or not. What I can say is I feel terribly for her and immediately edit her byline to a pseudonym and hope it blows over. It does not. Commenters notice the change in name and it only adds fuel to their astonishing need to vomit vitriol into the comment section.

Finally the trolls get bored with this particular target and move on. The writer later contacts me to say she has been re-hired. But things don't move on quite as quickly for me. The whole episode - the nature of the piece itself, my reaction to the reaction - is questioned and I receive the most serious rebuke of my tenure at CNN. I've received admonishing emails before and always respond with a defense, often fueled by a few beers, that I often wish I had kept to myself. The crimes are never that serious and I feel that all involved know these are simply the stepping-stones we had to tread as part of a large bureaucratic organization.

But this time the reprimand feels much more like an official warning to be noted on my record. Frustratingly, it also arrives in my inbox the day before I'm due to hold my wedding reception dinner. Andrew Demaria, who sits just across from me, pings it out around 5.30 pm on the Friday, saying as he does so "Not the best timing mate, but had to send you this." I decide to ignore it till after the weekend.

The next Monday, now an officially married man, I read it through. It's a huge, bullet point-by-bullet point reproof of my work on that feature, from the salacious headline, to the content in the piece, to the changing of the byline, also sidestepping into vague points about protecting writers and upholding the CNN brand.

I read it once only, quell my urge to respond with a similar point-by-point defense of everything mentioned, and hit delete. Part of me thinks Demaria is just going through the corporate playbook, doing what protocol says should be done in circumstances such as these. But I also know he's personally embarrassed, again, at having to explain content we publish to the bigwigs in Atlanta and London. The ad sales guys are having a much heavier influence on what we should and shouldn't do now, and if the sales guys aren't on your side, you won't make your revenue targets and you can be sure it won't be long before your provocative little site is shuttered up. We need to be playing the right game in the right way, and this kind of content - or at least the reaction we see to this post - would have caused some consternation for those trying to support and sell the merits of CNN Travel to a paying client base.

15 PLAGIARISM AND THE 5 COMMANDMENTS

Barely a week passes without some journalist being outed on Twitter as a thief. Plagiarism - the term for editorial burglary - is the top no-no for writers who want a long-term career.

My five commandments for travel writers - it's not a complicated business, we don't need ten - are:

1. Don't plagiarize
2. File copy on time
3. Fact check your copy
4. Report, don't sell
5. Source images

So when one of my key writers was found to have used someone else's text, I was genuinely disappointed. She was the list writer I mentioned in chapter 9, who wrote 32 articles for me in 18 months. You might consider her crime fairly minor - she was found to have used PR copy from a company's website in an article without attribution. It wasn't even a full sentence, but half a sentence. I know for a fact this goes on across the industry every day, thousands of times, to a far greater degree, with zero complaints. Some will even argue that pasting PR copy from a company's marketing materials is doing exactly what that company wants you to do. There's no author to credit with this kind of prose and the company certainly isn't going to chase after you with a lawsuit.

So this may not have been a crime against commandment number 1 above. But it was a crime against commandment number 4, and against the objective, journalistic standards required of anyone working for CNN. So the same day the misdemeanor was discovered, I was instructed to delete all but one or two of this writer's articles from the site. The executive editor wrote the writer a fairly terse email explaining the issues, and after some back and forth from the writer arguing her innocence, the matter was closed.

Admittedly, I struggled with this decision internally. I knew why the supervising eds above me had made it and I didn't argue. It probably didn't help that several high profile plagiarism cases were making headlines at around the same time - particularly that of Fareed Zakaria, a CNN broadcaster and Time columnist. He was suspended from duties while investigations took place, and reinstated just a week later. But when a partnership like this writer's and mine dissolves, you can't help but feel a little sorry. Not least because I was now stuck without my premier pageview driver, and needed to find another quick.

1. Don't plagiarize

Editorial theft works in the other direction too. Frequently I would find pieces we had published ripped off and loaded up onto suspicious blogs and sites. I would inform the executive eds who would inform legal, who would write menacing letters threatening legal action unless the offending material was immediately removed. It rarely worked.

People ripped off my own work on occasion too. In August 2013 I wrote a piece entitled "Why I hate museums". There was a fair amount of lip-chewing and brow-furrowing in the days leading up to publish date by the senior execs who were concerned the negative vibe of the piece might not be in CNN's best interests. Ad sales teams have a lot of power in large media corporations, and if they worry the content going up might turn off potential clients, we all have to relent.

On this occasion however the piece was given the green light and it went up. And it took off. Within 48 hours the piece had generated hundreds of comments, thousands of social media shares, and most pleasingly of all for me, dozens of spin-off blog posts by other writers adding to the debate.

I'm pretty sure to date the piece will have generated more than a million pageviews, which is unusual for an op-ed. Many, perhaps most, of the comments and spin-off blog posts were calling me out as an idiot, an ignoramus, a narrow-minded imbecile who should just go back to watching Honey-Boo-Boo videos on YouTube. For the record, the first I ever heard of Honey-Boo-Boo was in these comments. I had tried to preempt these accusations in the piece, by stating:

"...there's a climate of snobbery surrounding this whole industry. Confess that rather than stare glumly at an old beer chalice on a plinth you'd prefer to drink happily from a shiny new one in a pub, and you risk being outed as an ignoramus."

Obviously that failed. But it didn't matter to me. After several years writing deliberately provocative opinion pieces, these comments just drifted off into the ever-expanding ocean of critical Internet comments I witnessed every day. My skin had grown tough.

In fact, as we know, I encouraged them. The whole point of writing pieces like this was to generate interaction with readers, to stimulate debate, to engage. Exactly the kinds of things that I argued museums lacked. In that sense, this was probably the most successful piece I wrote during my tenure at CNN. I received an expenses-paid invitation to speak at a museum conference in Germany off the back of this one piece. I spoke (via video) at the California Association of Museums annual meet-up. And I had the pleasure of seeing many people continue to debate and argue and write about this topic. You cannot ask for much more than that from a single op-ed.

And so, when a year later I saw a mainstream newspaper

website in the UK had published a piece with exactly the same angle, and several very similar points and arguments inside the piece, I was pretty pissed off. I tweeted, sarcastically, to the editor who wrote that piece: "Thanks for finally editing my piece on museums". He tweeted back: "I don't follow".

I would never be able to prove anything as serious as plagiarism in this case. Plagiarism occurs when exact words have been copied, and his piece was his own writing, even if the core idea, as well as several points inside the piece, was originally mine. So I let it go. And, as I knew from a similar occurrence a few months earlier, you cannot copyright an idea.

It was February 2013, and I published a piece titled "Why the 'white tax' is perfectly acceptable". Yes, another deliberately provocative post, but an argument that I genuinely believed, at least mostly. This was a counter-argument to the complaint so many travelers make when visiting particularly Asian tourist attractions, that they get charged more than locals for the same experience. Look the piece up online to read it through (you can look all these posts up online in fact, by searching for the headline and my surname). It was another enjoyable piece, nowhere near as viral as the museums piece, but good fun to research and write and with enough reader comments to give me that sense of satisfaction that comes from seeing people engage with your writing - even if they're trying to smash it to a pulp.

Then, in September that same year, a blogger whose

mailing list I was on sent out his weekly newsletter, with a piece along exactly the same lines. The angle was the same, many of his points within the argument were the same, even some of the illustrative examples he used to color his piece were nearly identical. His only get-out, like the museums piece, was that there was no word-for-word cut-and-pasting plagiarism apparent.

I asked Chuck Thompson, an experienced editor and author, if there was anything I could do in these circumstances and his message was essentially no - you're going to have to live with it. Consider it an homage or a compliment, he said, that he liked your piece enough to want to do a cover version. And also be content in the knowledge that yours is a far superior piece.

I think what most galled me was even after I wrote to the blogger, mainly to let him know I had seen his piece and was not happy, and he returned some rather anxious-sounding rebuttals, he then went on to submit the piece for a travel writing competition and, in forums I was a member of too, petitioned fellow writers to vote for his post.

Is there a message here? I'm not sure. If there is it seems to be that writers can copy other writers whenever they like, and as long as they don't plagiarize can get out of jail by playing the you-inspired-me card.

Michael Kinsley wrote a very nice piece in Vanity Fair about this issue, particularly concerning Fareed Zakaria, the CNN and Time correspondent and columnist, who was suspended for a week in 2012 while accusations were investigated. He was reinstated. Kinsley writes:

"Plagiarism is the theft of other people's words or ideas. Just half a dozen identical words in two different works of literature is enough to create a legitimate suspicion. Theft of ideas is the worse crime—words are easy to come by; ideas are not."

And adds later:

"Any writer who is not a reckless egomaniac lives in fear of accidentally using some phrase that he or she admired and that planted itself in his or her brain. You can claim it's an accident or coincidence and maybe get away with it. But words that are slightly different can't be that way accidentally. They must be part of a conscious attempt to mislead."

His entire piece is worth reading to get a sense of how difficult it is to be original these days, or, perhaps more apropos, how difficult it is to *appear* to be original.

The bewildering thing is that plagiarism continues even in the age of the Internet, when it's so easy to discover. Not only is "plagiarism checker" software available, Google search itself is as good a tool as any for checking suspicious copy. Particularly with new freelancers I've commissioned, I'll often paste random sentences or phrases from their filed copy into Google and see what results. I've caught a few this way, and though I have a two-strikes policy, many don't.

The risk of being outed these days is so much higher, given the Internet's ability to seek and destroy, and when you are, it's forever and it can be brutal. Many large media platforms are keen to be seen as putting editorial integrity foremost, often with potentially career-killing public statements. CNN did it here [URL: http://edition.cnn.com/2014/05/16/world/editors-note/], The Guardian did it here [URL: https://www.theguardian.com/commentisfree/2016/may/26/open-door-column-note-to-readers], and there are more besides.

2. File copy on time

I probably don't really need to explain why each of these commandments makes my list. They are the fundaments of being a pro. But let me add a line or two just to explain from the editor's perspective.

When writing for a print publication, timeliness is paramount. Late copy can delay printing, which can incur fines for the publisher. That's the argument, anyway. In reality back-up stories will be available or hastily created to avoid the fines. But you should still file your copy by a specified date, because you agreed to.

That argument holds for online writing too. There are no printers in web world and in truth a single late article isn't going to cripple a publication. They will also have fill-ins to fall back on. But websites often have traffic targets, which your piece may impact, and many posts these days are tied to time-bound events.

Conclusion: file your copy on time, because it's good manners and could affect the publisher's business. If you don't you'll piss off your editor and may potentially affect his or her inclination to use you again.

3. Fact check your copy

Hopefully no extensive explanation needed here either. Ask any editor or experienced writer what the single most important quality a journalist can aspire to is, and he or she will reply: accuracy. Accuracy provides integrity, to your writing, your articles and yourself.

You don't want to be the writer editors talk about in meetings with a wince and a sneer, saying, "Yes we could use her, but she'll need extensive fact checking. Anyone else available?"

4. Report, don't sell

Another facet of your integrity. If you want to be a proper travel writer, that means describing the world honestly and accurately so others can form opinions on whether to go or not. However lucky you feel to be there, however grateful you are to the company who gave you a cut-price press rate, however many other gushing, effusive, promotional articles you've read in in-flight magazines and travel-agent-bound brochures, you are a professional and objectivity is elemental.

Many starting out in travel writing feel the need to think of themselves as exactly that – "travel writers". In fact there's no such thing as travel writing, there is only writing, and your subject happens to fall into the travel genre. The problem with being a "travel writer" is you could fall victim to what Martin Amis calls "herd (or heard?) writing" – trying to write how you think a travel writer should write (based on all the "travel articles" you've read to date). This can lead to pieces full of clichés and the kind of fluffy, quaint prose designed to sell places and destinations, rather than report on them.

5. Source images

I don't imagine this will be a popular commandment, but it pays to be willing to provide or source pictures along with your copy these days.

The Internet has forced previously distinct roles together. While newspapers used to have (some still do) the luxury of staffing themselves up with editors, roving editors, editors-at-large, editors in chief, section editors, writers, copy editors and whoa, even photo editors, as well as photographers, illustrators and graphic designers, I don't know of any web platform that retains all these roles. In most cases, a single online editor does all this now, perhaps with a junior staffer to help out.

So anything you can do to make the editor's job easier will help you stand out.

Freelance writing is a competitive field, and those of us

keen to pursue it need to ask ourselves: how can I make myself more valuable to an editor? How do I stand apart from the sea of pitches and wannabe writers clamoring for their attention? How do I retain a spot in the front of their mind when they ask themselves: who's a good writer for this job?

The answer, as painful as it may sound, is to do more, to offer extra, to make the editor's job easier, which means, in this example, supplying pictures along with your copy.

I've assigned to hundreds of writers over the last several years, and the ones that I turned to most often were the ones willing to source photography. Two in particular weren't the greatest writers I've ever assigned to, but one always filed good PR shots with her pieces and the other came in a tag-team duo where she wrote the articles and her photographer boyfriend supplied pics, as a package deal. They didn't ask for it, but I gave them a slightly higher fee than average simply because they offered this quality package.

Sure, sourcing photography is more work, it'll take more time, and you may not even get paid more. But that's how this trade is changing.

And you can be sure if you flat out refuse to source pics there's another writer in line who will be willing to do so. Just as an editor needs to write, edit, sub, upload and commission stories these days, so a freelancer should be willing to provide or source pictures.

16 INSIDE CNN: WHEN IT GOES RIGHT

Content really is king. There's no better way to market, brand, sell or distribute than simply publishing good content. The other stuff always helps, but it's icing compared to the cake.

Salacious headlines, pictures of sexy people, social media marketing and distribution, celeb/influencer endorsements, clever techy A/B tests, clever techy SEO tweaks - it's all clickbait, really, because it's all gloss, an attempt to convince people to click your post rather than someone else's, through presentation.

And yes, I count myself among those who participate to some degree. I churn out lists at CNN Travel like my livelihood depends on them. And in a way it does. In Chapter 3 we saw some of the listicle headlines I published that did extremely well, click-wise. And here are some more that didn't make the top 50:

10 of the world's best nighttime adventures

8 greatest city mascots around the world
12 game-changing theme park attractions
9 of the world's most controversial foods
8 vending machines you didn't know you needed
5 hotels for chocoholics
Best airport restaurants around the world
World's 10 most spectacular university buildings
World's scariest, best water slides
Around the world in 11 odd cheeses
9 of the world's greatest tunnels
10 hotels featured in James Bond movies
Postcards vs. the future: 10 endangered travel items
13 scary-but-awesome viewing platforms
Bye-bye Bora Bora - 15 other islands in French Polynesia
12 of the world's dog-friendliest hotels
7 trips for 7 travelers
15 greatest hats of the world
World's 10 best cities for foodies

There are probably a couple hundred more list posts I can add to my "assigned" portfolio. You may read down the list above and think, "That sounds quite interesting actually. I'd click that."

And you probably would. You may be headed to French Polynesia soon and genuinely want to know about the lesser-visited islands there. You may be an engineer and be intrigued to see which tunnels made our list. You may be a cheese fanatic and simply love reading everything you can find about cheese. You may simply have five minutes to kill and give in to the lure of the listicle headline.

My point is not that these are awful topics that should never see the light of day. Nor that they should never be read. I defended lists some pages back and stand by it - they are extremely useful, valuable pieces of content that are proven traffic builders, and anything that builds traffic helps gets ads, which keeps us all in business. And I assign hundreds of them after all. But giving topics the listicle treatment day after day, week after week, does any site a disservice and I'm trapped inside a listicle mindset.

This is why print magazines still hold a valuable place in the travel-writing kingdom. Lists and quick-fix reads have proliferated on the Internet because of the nature of that medium. The Internet is a lean-forward platform. You read online content to gain something or to learn and once you've achieved your goal you click away.

Print magazines offer the lean-back approach, where you soak up the words and the pictures and the story and the characters slowly, fully, perhaps in an armchair with a cup of coffee or glass of wine. There's no rush with a magazine or a book. The physical nature of the thing, the sensory experience, the noise of the pages turning, flipping, wrinkling, the smell of the ink, the colors, the fonts, the graphics, add up to something that's comfortable and sometimes even comforting. The Internet, peered at on bright screens on hard-edged desks or hard to hold phones or tablets is a distinctly less comfortable experience, something one feels one needs get away from as soon as possible.

And so, what the articles named above and many others like them do, is provide quick, tasty morsels that you can enjoy while you're reading them, but can then be instantly forgotten. There are few takeaways. You don't learn much from them, they don't unravel mysteries, there's no narrative, they're not useful in any way - they are, at core, entertainments rather than journalistic endeavors. Listicles are the fast-food buffets of the content world. Fatty, sugary and salty, hitting all the top flavor spots with each bite, but you shouldn't live on them.

Well, that's true for most list content*. You can create worthy, high quality, journalistic list content if you put the work in. That means treating each item in the list like its own little article, requiring proper research, interviews, proper fact checking, quality writing and so on. One such example that I assign is "Asia's 10 greatest street food cities". This is a bit of a beast, picking out 10 cities famed for their street foods, giving brief intros to each, listing out 10 dishes for each city and even providing maps of walking routes to get to each of those dishes. A bona fide food writer who either knew these cities (and their food credentials) herself personally, or knew people who knew them, wrote the piece.

And it was a hit. It's nice to know that readers appreciate quality work when you go to the trouble. I can't recall the exact number of pageviews but it would have been a million plus, and in the top five stories for CNN Travel for a few months I expect.

Chuck Thompson assigned another to an ex-CNNer who was living in Germany. The piece was titled "Where's the Berlin Wall now? 10 surprising locations". To the list-fatigued, half-open eye, this could look like just another list piece identifying museum exhibits or personal collector items. But Google that headline and read it yourself - it's a proper piece of travel journalism, with history, context, intrigue, interviews, research and a genuinely novel treatment of a feature about one of 20th-century Europe's most historic icons.

A novel treatment or angle is one key to a proper piece of journalistic content. Two series I conceived during my last year or so I was particularly pleased with, not because they got away from the list format (they didn't) nor because they were amazing pieces of ground-breaking journalism (they weren't), but because they did offer something different to the usual list formula (number + superlative + thing + place = clicks) I described back in Chapter 3. These series contained pieces with headlines like:

10 things to know before visiting Sweden
and
10 things Canada does better than anywhere else

Each of these ideas had ten to fifteen articles assigned against them, simply substituting in different countries each time. And they drove millions of pageviews. Their click-worthy ingredient is their nationalistic vibe - both kinds of pieces were greedily gobbled down by readers in the countries featured, firstly because they were keen to see what CNN had to say about their home, but also because media in those countries also picked up on the pieces for exactly the same reason.

And here we finally get to the point of this chapter. Three of the four 'scandalous' posts I described in Chapter 14 blew up because media in some of the featured countries picked up and ran their own editorials on our posts. Their readers then joined the fray, the ripples became waves and we thrashed and tumbled in the froth.

HOW TO SELL TRAVEL STORIES

But it does work in the other direction too, when media pick up on 'what CNN said about us' in a positive light.

--

* I do know many writers don't like to use or hear the word "content," as if the collective noun for their stories somehow diminishes the art within. I use the word to refer to all articles, posts, videos, podcasts, news stories, galleries, features etc, so I don't have to write up that lengthy list each time.

*

TALKING EDS

Francisca Kellett, travel editor, TATLER magazine

Worst pitch?

"Hi! I've been invited on a press trip to the Maldives, and have always wanted to go to the Maldives, so please will you commission me? xx" Bad pitches usually follow a similar pattern – someone I don't know who has been invited on a bog standard press trip which I've probably already declined, and they really fancy a jolly drinking cocktails in the sun. And do your research: crimes that deserve instant deleting include pitching something that we've just run, pitching an idea that isn't appropriate for my readers, and pitching something which was obviously first pitched to a competitor – you'd be amazed how often people forget to change the name of an editor or publication before hitting 'send'. And please don't sign off with kisses unless we have actually kissed in real life.

Perfect pitch?

Yup, lots - they are from those clever types who have researched the kind of articles and reviews we run, checked if we've already covered something, and pitched the right kind of story, angle or property. If the email makes me laugh out loud, you'll get a gold star.

Assigns?

An understanding of the readership, and a sense of humor.

Writing goals?

Make them laugh (which is harder than it sounds). In general, travel writing can take itself terribly seriously – 'serious' pieces have their place, of course, but in general it's always best to entertain and amuse while you do that whole "inspirational" thing...

--

@frankellett and www.tatler.com

17 TOPICS (NOT) TO PITCH

If we tack away from the angle of the pitch for a moment, we can consider the story. What kinds of stories should writers be looking for and then pitching to editors?

There's no single answer to that, which is a good thing. Every magazine has its own audience, every editor his or her own preferences and idiosyncrasies. It's easier to describe the stories I get tired of seeing and am unlikely to assign.

Disclaimer: just because I wouldn't assign a particular story, or set of stories, doesn't mean all editors think the same, even those who worked with me at the same time at CNN.

Subjects that get pitched more than any others, and are likely either already done by the publication, or simply tedious to read about for the 45th time, are an easy one to avoid. This is why research into the publication should be done before you pitch. Your story about the Amazonian tribe that offers AirBnB stays to travelers may be great, but it won't go anywhere if your target publication ran the same piece last week or last month. It's too easy to run a quick search online these days to fall at this hurdle.

Using a publication's archive can also be a good way of finding old stories the editor may want updated or totally rewritten. If your guide to Seoul's newest restaurants has already been done, but was posted five years ago, it's well worth pitching with some examples of how you'll update their info.

So what topics do I tire of seeing?

Spas. Every travel writer and her daughter have been to a wonderful spa that absolutely must be written about. Too easy and too dull. Unless there really is a story to be told, I don't ever assign spa stories any more. Certainly not vanilla reviews anyway. Give me a tale of how the spa turned its remote Thai village into a hub for reflexology training, or how the spa manager lives a second life as a drag queen at weekends, or how the spa's built on the location of an ancient Mayan temple, and I might be intrigued.

Restaurant reviews. There are places for restaurant reviews, but I never assign them unless, again, there's a cracker of a story inside.

Hotel openings. If you're writing about a hotel opening

and only a hotel opening, you're a PR machine, not a travel writer. What I'd want from a story based on a hotel opening is some context and expert opinion on how this opening will affect the area, the travelers, the city, the world, in a way that merits a story. Or a spotlight on something truly interesting, perhaps even unique, about the place.

Any single venue reviews. A lot of titles run reviews of restaurants, hotels, cafes, etc. as a regular feature. I don't mean to say there isn't a place for them, but that place is best inside a local newspaper or magazine. To date, I've worked with international platforms trying to cover six, sometimes seven continents, which means giving space to a single venue in a piece, possibly the only piece we run that day, is a tall ask unless, again, there's a real story to be told.

Plus, it's all too obvious when I get a pitch declaring this fantastic hotel via a bunch of puffy PR graphs, probably lifted straight from the hotel's own website, that the writer is looking for some cheap or free accommodation at their next destination city. If you must write about restaurants or hotels, I'd be much more inclined to assign if the pitch was for a list of some kind (10 funniest themed restaurants in Canada, China's craziest hotel designs)

24/48/72 hours in [Rome]. I've yet to see an X hours in Y article that didn't appear to be written by Superman jacked up on speed. If I'm in a city for 48 hours I congratulate myself if I order room service only twice. Yes these pieces invariably tell you to hit a museum, a cafe, a new art exhibition and take a river stroll all before lunch. A cute treatment of a bunch of listings basically, which is putting style before substance.

Finally one way not to write: the imperative. This comes courtesy of Chuck Thompson, who drilled it into our heads at CNN and to date I've not found a reason to disagree. The imperative voice is the voice of so many travel publications and writers. It's the voice of casual and therefore lazy authority, of manufactured intimacy, of writing as you've seen things written before.

It's particularly pervasive in pieces such as "24 hours in Rome", where the writer will command his reader to do stuff. "Take a wander through the meandering streets before hitting Coffee Coma, the newest cafe on the block. Order a Coffeecino - you won't be disappointed. Make sure you use the bathroom on the left for a surreal view of the Tiber, then head out again and peruse the shops that line the walkway back down into town."

First of all this is not a pleasant way to write - because it's not a pleasant way to read. But even if you disagree with that, even if you think the imperative works (which it can in some rare cases) you must also agree that it's common and standard. Thompson said: If we want to stand out from the crowd we can't write like the crowd.

18 INSIDE CNN: LAYOFFS

In July 2010, with Kim Willis no longer with the project, Chuck Thompson, an author, former editor in chief of Travelocity magazine, former features editor at Maxim and already with one stint at CNNGo on his CV, returns as editorial director.

Over the next 18 months he oversees the editorial expansion of CNNGo, including the addition of two new cities to our existing six and the launch of four local language sites, in Japanese, Korean and both Simplified and Traditional Chinese.

In January 2012 he sends this email:

> **From: Thompson, Chuck**
> **To: Durston, James + 10 others**
> **SUBJ: Yesterday, Today and Tomorrow**

> Go Team:

I can't help but add a few thoughts of my own here. For the most part, Andrew is comfortable allowing me to speak for him in these situations but I'm leaving Andrew off of this email because I'd like to explain and address a few things that are sensitive areas for him.

First off, I want to let you all know that Andrew is in a tough spot right now in which he is compelled to keep his mouth shut about things he doesn't like or agree with. I'm talking about decisions that have been made about everything from losing staff to how the site will move ahead.

I think you can all imagine the process, but to spell it out, the discussions that led to today's drama began a few months ago when Peter Bale entered the picture from CNN in London and, more recently, Phil Nelson took over for Yew Ming. (Surprise, right?!)

There have also been discussions with people in Atlanta. CNNGo has been under scrutiny, but under even more scrutiny have been our accounting ledgers.

These discussions were at times very contentious. I have not been privy to all of them, but I have been privy to some of them and had one or two of my own. I want to let you guys know that Andrew has fought tooth and nail on behalf of this edit staff. I would like to say what little contributions I have made to this effort have been in full alignment with AD.

I hope you all know me at least well enough to know by now that I'm no bootlicker, but I can say with all honesty that I have been, and I know you all would be, very proud of the job Andrew has done in arguing convincingly to higher ups on all of our behalves. We have allies very high in this company -- they like Andrew, they respect him -- he has done well at maneuvering us through this company shit storm.

As they say in the sports, AD's is the sort of contribution that "doesn't show up in the box scores." It's also been a huge stress on the guy. We really do owe him a round of thanks.

That said, as you all well know, once a decision is made, it is incumbent upon any manager to support the decisions and directives of those above him.

Andrew is now in the unenviable position that all managers hate -- breaking news and carrying out a few measures that he doesn't necessarily love. If AD answers your questions in a way that seems vague or non-committal, if he does not seem forthcoming with all of his thoughts, this is likely why.

You should re-read the first part of this letter and consider giving him the benefit of the doubt if you are frustrated by his inability to always be completely candid.

A few other thoughts:

Two staffers mentioned to me that laying off people and breaking this bad news on the cusp of Chinese New Year was very poor form. Although I am honorary Chinese, I'm obviously not Chinese enough to fully grasp the bad vibes this has generated with some of you but I will say I agree with you, the thought also crossed my mind, and I am sorry.

There's nothing we can do about it now, this is a big, unforgiving company, it doesn't give a shit about protocol, but it is an embarrassment and I feel sorry that it is affecting some people in this way. The company may not care, but the people in front of you every day very much do. On behalf of CNN/Turner/CNNGo, I'm sorry.

To me, losing five good edit staffers is plain and simple a failure on behalf of myself. I'm not saying this to garner sympathy or support. Don't tell me it's OK. It's my job to make the edit of this site work and make this a good place for people to work and have security and do good work and take care of this so that AD doesn't have to worry about the edit part of the equation. I still do believe content is king and we are nothing without good content.

The solution now is to re-double efforts to make this site succeed, but I know the psychic turmoil these layoffs cause and I want to apologize to all of you for allowing it to happen. It fucking hurts to lose people who cared about their jobs as much as our colleagues did, and who I personally liked as much as I liked all those guys who lost jobs today. It's fucking heartbreaking.

That said, I think CNNGo is actually about to make some very important and smart strides toward being more relevant to readers and we can all feel better about what the site is to become.

As some of you know who talk to me more than others, I have always maintained that the "city-centric" focus was idiotic -- a really dumb business model from day one. I'm thrilled that we are going to abandon it.

I am thrilled because I believe it will make us more relevant to more readers and help the site make some actual sense. CNNGo grew out of the imagination of an insane woman and the more we distance ourselves from her insane ideas, the better chance we have for success. This is a HUGE and positive step.

I'm excited about it.

Local language: When AD asked me to come back to the site in July 2010, one of the main reasons I said yes was because I was excited about the possibility of the local language sites really breaking open some doors for us.

It didn't happen. Personally, I'm inclined to blame a severe lack of marketing efforts for our LL [local language] sites and a misunderstanding by non-LL speakers in our organization about what the situations were in our 4 LL markets.

But all of that is speculation and sour grapes. What is good and important is that we have managed to retain three excellent and valued LL editors and I want you guys to know that just because your sites will go fallow, does not mean your best contributions to this site have ended.

In fact, I believe your best work might just be beginning.

At the same time, I want to express to you three LL editors how much I know it hurts to lose the sites you have babied into existence. Tracy, that goes for you, too, who started the Shanghai LL site. This hurts to lose and there's no point hiding from that fact.

There's also no point wallowing in it.

Success: There was a great emphasis on sales and blaming sales in today's meeting. I want to say that I think sales does deserve some blame for our predicament, but not all of it.

We have over-reached as a business. When someone tells us (as Phil Nelson did at that start of that call) that we spent $3 million this year while only bringing in $1 million, that suggests to me some pretty big cost overruns that should not have happened. And I think we can all figure out the approximate salary of everyone on this email and understand that it ain't just paycheck accounting for $2 mil shortfall.

Fact is, we are in this position today because the business side of things -- not just sales -- hasn't been handled well at all.

Although I hate the loss in people we took today, I hate losing our LL sites, I'm extremely gratified that someone is finally starting to take us seriously as a business. That is GREAT news in the long run. I've been waiting for this since the day I started working here in July 2009. About fucking time.

Personally, even accounting for his tough spot introduction, I don't think Phil Nelson came across well to most of us today. He gave us a lot of corporate bullshit.

But I don't think we should write him off just yet. For one thing, he's here, he's guiding the ship now, so we have to deal with him. But for another, I actually think the guy knows what he is doing and can get us on a better path toward not showing a fucking $2 mil loss when we are exceeding traffic goals. Let's give this guy a shot.

But listen guys, please: We are not sales and we cannot let sales begin to dictate overmuch what we do as editors and writers. Yes, we need sales to survive, yes, it is part of our business. But that is not our part -- our part is to put out great copy and that is all.

Believe me, you don't want to go down the road of custom publishing for clients. I have spent the last two months basically working for fucking Delta and MasterCard pretty much because we have needed these projects to survive, we have needed to prove to London and ATL that we can generate revenue.

But I'm about to slash my wrists with boredom and, anyway, the content we do for them will not drive much traffic (some will, most won't) and it is not the kind of stuff we all became journos or editors or writers to do.

At the end of the day, our final and only real measure of success has to be how proud we are of the copy we produce, sales or not. And if we all get fired in the end, if we're proud of the copy we've produced, we get to go out with our swords in hands and our shields up, so let's not forget that our money and jobs are not the same things as our work and our reputations. The latter is much more important, will last longer and carry us to more places.

I know there are lots of questions about the new edit strategy for CNNGo. AD will address that next week. I think it's positive.

For right now I just wanted to give us a forum to speak a little bit frankly -- fuck, does that corporate "transparent" non-speak make anyone else as sick as it does me? I feel like puking about all of this, I feel like we deserve better and I think we've got a chance to get it.

Is all of this just spin or rationalization by me, trying to put some shine on a dog turd? Maybe a little, yeah, but I guess that's natural.

I do think we should all be a lot sad today, and a lot pissed off, but come back next week doing what we know will work if we stick to it and clear a few more obstacles out of our way.

Thanks for letting me purge guys, please don't pass this around, I know this ain't elegant, I wish we were all together for beers and bitching, maybe this is my way of doing it, respond if you like, ignore me if not, talk next week, enjoy that Monday off.

Chuck

19 COMPS, FAMS AND JUNKETS

I need to take a moment to touch on the sensitive topic of basing stories on complimentary press trips, FAMs, free hotel rooms and the like. Some publications (CNN Travel, The New York Times, Travel + Leisure, Huffington Post) maintain policies not to run stories that result from subsidized trips or experiences, reasoning that the writing may be influenced by the generosity of the subject, or, even if it isn't, that readers may surmise it is. I think this is a mistake and many of us at CNN Travel thought so too. We petitioned to get the rule changed to no avail.

Nonetheless, I also had the sense that this was a rule to be seen and heard by people who mattered (readers, especially) but not necessarily followed to the letter. I was given, unofficially, flexibility on this rule when I managed a sponsored series of content on "Elite Escapes" - trips costing thousands of dollars each that no freelancer could

128

be expected to cover. I suspect at least a few other regular features were also "cost assisted", despite the policy forbidding freebies being explicitly addressed in the writer guidelines. I wrote a couple of pieces myself that were the result of trips that charged "media-rated" fees - CNN was charged 50% of the regular rate.

Why is having a "no comps" policy problematic? For precisely the reason the rule was flexed when CNN had something to gain - namely a lucrative sponsored content deal. It can mean you miss out, on both content and revenue. Had I followed the rule to the letter for Elite Escapes the content wouldn't have been anywhere near as good, our pageviews possibly would have sagged and any chance of impressing the client (and winning a renewal of the sponsorship) would have been tainted if not lost.

Content-wise, say Richard Branson wants to generate buzz for Virgin Galactic's first commercial space flight by sending journalists on a complimentary preview trip. If you discount your publication because of a no-comps policy, you either shell out the US$250,000 fee or you miss out on the biggest travel story of the century.

Publications besides CNN know this; the BBC even states in its writer guidelines that it does not accept stories based on comps, "except in the rare case in which it is the only opportunity for press to be a part of something before the public launch, it is the only way to gain access to something or the story would be logistically unattainable otherwise."

So, as a non-negotiable rule, the no-comps policy can be a

major drawback. However, push it too far the other way and you risk discrediting everything you should stand for as a journalist.

A lot of noise has been made of this in recent months, with bloggers and other social media "influencers" attracting spotlights. The UK's Competition and Markets Authority has warned social media celebrities and other digital stars that endorsing products without declaring they had been paid to do so could be a breach of consumer protection law. The US Federal Trade Commission announced a similar regulation in 2009. Disclosure is one thing. But social media celebs and influencers can hardly be considered journalists. They're marketers and brand ambassadors (the "brands" most often being themselves) and could arguably be given greater latitude than someone whose professional mission is to impart accurate, truthful and verifiable information.

But what of bloggers and travel writers? Whenever I've heard travel writers discuss this topic, nearly all say with impressive intent that though they accept junkets and comps, it never influences their writing, they're professionals, they have more integrity than that. My problem with this is whether you can be absolutely sure you aren't censoring yourself, or gushing, even unconsciously.

If you're a travel writer who relies on junkets and comped experiences because that's the only way you can afford to go places and do things worth writing about, you'd be a fool to start gnawing at the hand that feeds you. If junkets comprise a minor deviation or an occasional treat, you're probably doing fine. If they make up every trip you take and every experience you write about, you may need to rethink things. And I've seen at least one writer proudly boast of not writing for money, but for the trips. That's a luxury very few of us can afford and probably results in articles even fewer of us should want to read.

The question you need to ask is: who are you serving when you accept a comped trip or product? If you're serving either yourself or the company that's offering the comp first, then you can't expect to be taken seriously as a travel writer. At the very least you can't call yourself a journalist. But if you're genuinely serving the reader, and the comp is a means to an end (that end being a great story) then good for you. Keep at it.

20 INSIDE CNN: THE METAMORPHOSIS

In November 2012, CNNGo becomes CNN Travel. We've been anticipating this transition for more than a year. It's been spun to us as a good thing. Notwithstanding the loss of staff earlier in the year, this will give us more reach, greater distribution, more traffic, more sponsors, more money and more kudos with the CNN execs that matter. We're even allotted our own permanent space on the CNN.com homepage, along with a "Travel" navigation tab atop the page, a great coup for a struggling platform.

It all sounds like a great success, that the last three to four years of work have paid off, that this is the promised land and we have arrived.

But it's also clear that CNNGo as a project failed. The access to the content through the main CNN homepage is at the same time a total transformation of the CNNGo brand, personality and mission. The city-based structure has been eradicated in favor of a locale non-specific approach. The loss of the local language sites and the laying off of staff to a fraction of the peak number is further evidence that our little experiment, for all it's Facebook fans, all its traffic, all its month-on-month growth, hasn't worked out. That traffic counts for little if you're still spending more each year than you're earning. That our edgy, fluff-free, all-sides-of-the-story voice, drilled into us each week since Thompson returned, might be great for attracting clicks and social media follows from backpacking travelers and defiant millennials, but actually needs to attract big-spending sponsors and corporate partners.

It doesn't occur to me, nor I think the other editors and staff below the ranks of Demaria and Thompson, and that's no surprise. We've been doing our jobs, pumping out content, driving traffic, hitting targets. As far as we're concerned we're a huge success.

It's a testament to Demaria's political talents that not only has CNN has been willing to endure us, a minor department based in Asia that started as an experiment under CNN International, a small cog grinding away in the dark shadow of what we call CNN domestic (the US business), for this long already, but he's also managed to impart to us a sense of achievement and of being valued.

It didn't have to work out that way.

CNN has been publishing travel content for a decade or more before CNNGo comes along. It just doesn't have its own space with its own navigation tab on the main site. Run by two edit staff in the Atlanta office, CNN's travel content is a bit of a "we better do this, because it will look odd if we don't" deal. Then CNNGo comes along, based in Hong Kong, with a focus on high-traffic, engaging, clickable content out of Asia created by a team of 20+, at its peak. We push hard on social media and utilize SEO, both relatively new concepts to CNN at that time.

At first, given our experimental (not just travel) nature and Asia focus, it's unlikely the Atlanta team feels there's any overlap, let alone competition. But as our traffic grows and our strategy changes to ditch the city-based Asia focus and go after global hits, suddenly it's CNN International in Hong Kong versus CNN domestic in Atlanta. We're meant to be talking to and communicating with the guys over there regularly, building a travel brand together, they acting as US editors and us covering the rest of the world. But Chuck Thompson, who, being based in Portland, Oregon has the most regular contact with the US team, frequently voices concerns about the stability of our relationship with them and the ease of working with people who appear to be anxious and defensive about our growing success.

We're paving new ground here, showing what kind of travel content does well and how to fashion it, and I can easily imagine the Atlanta team, who have been running CNN's travel content for the last decade, whispering to each other with sneers on their faces about those impudent young upstarts over in the Orient thinking they know how to do OUR jobs. This simmering competition is frustrating, because as much as our traffic is growing month on month and we're building an audience loyal to our brand, there's one thing patently clear about where the real traffic comes from: CNN International's and CNN US's front pages.

When our content is placed by other CNN editors,

including those in Atlanta, on their pages, which receive multi-fold more visitors than our own mini-site, our traffic spikes. In fact, we come to rely more and more on the main CNN sites to keep our growth charting upwards. If left to fight for traffic only from our own corner of the CNN site we would flounder. So despite our frustrations we play nice with the US editors and hope it pays back in traffic. Later, these relationships improve and there's much more teamwork, as both sides of the world realize their interests are mutual and it's not a case of one or the other.

Convincing the Hong Kong editors to place our stories on the main CNN site is an easier task, where the relevant people sit just a floor above us now. We've been moved skywards again, like a metaphor for our rise into the CNN fold, to the 39th floor, just one story shy of the newsroom proper. If we can convince these editors that we have six or eight stories worth placing on their front page over the month, we know we'll hit yet another traffic record. So Demaria starts going to the news meetings every morning, to sell the merits of the pieces we're doing.

When he gets promoted, I take on this task. These news meetings take place first thing every morning, and are a chance for the reporters to share the stories they're chasing. Most times it pays off - the homepage producers are aware that our stories do well traffic-wise, and especially in the absence of a major breaking news event, they're grateful for that traffic - they have goals to meet too.

It's worth noting that while the Atlanta team seems to feel a little unnerved by our growth and success, we don't feel any analogous sense of triumph or security. We may be growing and we may be aiming for a transition from

CNNGo to CNN Travel, but we're also part of CNN International, a satellite of the core US business, with the levers mainly pulled in London, and the Hong Kong office a satellite of this satellite. So we're small fry, acknowledged like a first cousin's stepchild by those in the US, and we know it.

And until this point, there's been a cloud of doubt hanging over our heads regarding our perceived value within the company. We know we're doing a good job. Our traffic is high and growing every month. With Chuck Thompson guiding our editorial strategy and voice and Andrew Demaria ensuring we were sold politically across CNN, we've grown an audience and are being seen to have grown an audience.

But there's never any space to take things for granted. We're stuck out in Hong Kong, with most of the power in London or Atlanta, and there's always the sense that we're something of a nuisance out here, that the editorial and sales directors based in London and Atlanta would far prefer it if we were located alongside them, where they could 'guide' us easier.

The result is that we never feel set, and toward the end of every month the pressure is applied to get that little bit more, push that little bit harder, to make sure we earn our existence, unless we're over-hitting, in which case the reverse happens - slow down, we're told, let's manage our growth and the expectations of others.

But we've proven we can add value.

In March 2011 an earthquake off the coast of Japan devastates the area, killing 16,000 people. Demaria jumps at the opportunity to show the rest of CNN what this little travel outlet can do. While we write a couple of pieces in-house as minor news updates, it's our network of freelancers, many of whom live in Japan, that really stand us up. They write pieces that go all across the network, they act as stringers for the TV crews that travel over there and do their own to-camera reports as well. So given the right circumstances, we had editorial muscle worthy of the CNN brand.

But this is not our bread and butter, and we know it. The fact that we're invariably one of the top two departments in terms of monthly traffic numbers is a bonus, but almost incidental - the fear that lingers is fueled by politics and inter-departmental competition, not results.

But on November 13, 2012, all that came before is swept away and CNN Travel rises from the CNNGo ashes. For the last several weeks we've been readying the site technically for the transition. We're warned we may have to work the weekend. We're told to be on call for anything and everything that might occur. Facebook has been contacted to ensure our likes and follows on our main page transfer over. Unfortunately, all the likes on individual posts that migrate to the new CMS (and hence live under a new URL) will be lost.

The day comes, we're poised for the shit to not just hit the fan but splatter over the entire Hong Kong office ... but it all goes well. On our new front page an announcement post [URL: http://travel.cnn.com/ welcome-cnn-travel-248601/] is put in the top spot for a week. "While some CNNGo.com fans have expressed their sadness at seeing the site's unique name and branding retired, the new move is a positive one," the post says. "It represents a major commitment to a growth plan for 'travel' by CNN, and a considerable extension of the

CNNGo tagline, 'Local Insights, Global Experiences.'

"The familiar CNNGo focus, voice and concept are the same, but our coverage will now be carried out at a global level."

It's now the Asian city-focused presentation (in truth we've been doing a lot of international content already) is discarded, several of those city editors along with them, to instead retain a core team of Demaria and Thompson as overseers, with editors in charge of Asia, Europe, the Americas/Caribbean and "Homepage", and a mix of two to three staff writers and interns to help those editors with writing, image sourcing and uploading tasks.

The CNNGo voice is not far from the chopping block either, though it's not so much chopped off as slowly, sorely skinned, sliced and gutted until very little that's recognizable remains. This is the impact our success has - now the execs, having once struggled to know us, having seen the growth and the audience, decide it's time to monetize this brand by making it appeal to corporate sponsors. And that means making it safe, bland and personality-free. In effect, dialing down the Hunter S Thompson and dialing up the middle-class, empty-nester housewife/husband.

Where once we would have published a story such as "The best and worst flags of the world" or a review of a 3-D porn movie (yes, we did) without qualm or hesitation, now we pause. Now we worry what the bosses might think. The best/worst flags story is sent from the writer to me, to Thompson, to Demaria, to his boss in London, probably to the legal department in Atlanta and a few more before we get the feedback that it's too controversial, the worst flag inclusions too deliberately provocative, too negative. "I just don't see what the point is," is one of the comments from the London managing editor. Eventually that piece goes up under the headline "Raising the standard: Fascinating flags and the stories behind them" with any evaluative references (best, worst) removed, replaced with simple explainers on how certain flag designs came to be.

Needless to say this vanilarizing (my spellcheck here wants me to use "vandalizing" which wouldn't be totally inappropriate) of our content has been concerning Chuck Thompson and me for some time already.

Frequently in emails to Thompson lamenting the rounding off of our enjoyably edgy content, we end up conceding that sure, we may get pissed off at certain decisions sometimes but this is still a great gig. And we do occasionally find ways still to do great, fun work within these confines.

But now I start to question whether the best job I've ever had is as fun as I want to believe it is.

*

TALKING EDS

Tom Hall, editorial director, Lonely Planet

Worst pitch?

Any of the many that have made no effort to tell me why the story they're proposing is right for my audience. Self-centered writing is of no use whatsoever. At Lonely Planet we also get a lot of well-intentioned people getting in touch to say that they're going to X country and would we like anything? In the nicest possible way we'll never assign work in that way.

Perfect pitch?

I've seen some good ones, and on more than one occasion the writer has become a regular contributor, and even landed a staff job. For me it's no more than 50 words: what the feature is, why it's right for my publication and why the pitcher is the right person to write it. That's all.

Assigns?

As I've alluded to above, it's a focus on the taking the reader rather than the writer to the heart of the place. The other key thing I'm looking for is clean, succinct writing, preferably - and this is increasingly the norm - supported by superb images. I'm not looking for Paul Theroux or Patrick Leigh Fermor's style of travel writing. In a modern print and digital publication your writing has to be sharp and clean.

Writing goals?

The ultimate responsibility of a travel writer is to understand the obstacles between a would-be traveller making a successful journey, and showing them how to overcome it. People assume that being a travel writer is about going somewhere exotic and bashing out 1500 words about it. More often - and more valuable in my opinion - a travel writer will put together a well-written piece of travel advice.

I'm aiming for something different with every piece. At the moment given I'm in an in-house role I don't write as much as I have done in the past so I write to keep my hand in as much as anything.

--

Tom Hall is the editorial director at Lonely Planet and the author of Lonely Planet's Best Ever Travel Tips

21 BANNED WORDS AND TERMS

Every editor has their own semi-secret list of words and phrases that make them cringe. I'm making mine very public.

Doing something one meal/drink/suntan/basically any noun that isn't "step" at a time.
Something "boasting" something.
Gems - unless you're talking about rubies or diamonds, please tell me what you really mean.
Gorgeous - on a par with "nice" for meaninglessness.
Spectacular - as above.
Oasis of calm - if I had a penny for every time this has been written I wouldn't have bothered writing this book.
Bustling city - as above.
Resplendent.
Al fresco - you mean "outside" right?
The imperative - don't tell your reader what to do.

Cheers to that - so hackneyed, even if not used in a bar/drinks article.

Not all xxx are created equal.

For those brave enough to xxx - Almost always this features some humdrum activity such as "trying the local street food". We're not cowards.

Buzzing - for the most part, these kinds of words are non-words, because they could be applied to every example of whatever you're describing. Especially bees. And buzzers.

Colorful - as above.

Eatery - you mean "restaurant" right?

To die for - really?

Staycation/Daycation/Gaycation/Mancation.

Digital detox.

Puns - very occasionally a great pun can be conjured and the world becomes brighter. But for the most part, a quick Google of that great play on words you just invented will reveal a thousand other identical "inventions".

Off the beaten track - clichés work when speaking because they capture essence in few words. But when writing we need to aspire to be original.

For locals and visitors alike - So, everyone?

City of contrasts.

East meets West.

[City] is the [City] of the East/West/North/South.

Like stepping back in time.

22 INSIDE CNN: THE 40TH FLOOR

In September 2014, five years after launching as CNNGo and almost two years after metamorphosing into CNN Travel, we move to the heady heights of the 40th floor of Oxford House in Quarry Bay, Hong Kong, a building that has only 40 floors. This is our zenith, the top of the parabola.

Our staff, from a peak of nearly 20, has dwindled to nine. Traffic, which peaked at around 30 millions pageviews per month when Malaysia Airlines flight 370 went missing over the ocean in March 2014, has settled and stabilized around 25 million. The voice we established, grew up with and loved has been softened and smoothened, and we find ourselves well out of startup territory, hunkered down as a legitimate, permanent, accepted and acceptable part of the CNN brand proper. Or it appears so.

From the quaint little set up on the 29th, then the 33rd, then the 39th floor (we're bundled up and re-positioned on a higher floor three times in the five years I'm there), where the offices are stark and grey, bland and silent, a bona fide startup land where you had to be grateful for merely existing, the 40th floor feels like adventure and prestige and glory.

We're now bedded down with the newsreaders we see everyday on TV, the writers and journalists finding and making the news and all the accessories that go with. This is the real deal. This is what you imagine when you think of a busy, cross-platform, multimedia, multi-national news enterprise.

A double row of 22 TV monitors hangs over the director offices. Opposite, another ten TV screens are embedded into the CNN-red wall. Stage lights hang from the ceiling. The open-plan office stretches, desk beside desk, screen past screen, until your eye stops at the studio - more enormous TV screens, TV cameras, camera cranes, boom mikes and the anchor desk. Up here it feels live. Up here you can feel the world turning.

CNNGo, now CNN Travel, has made it. We can finally slip into cruise mode, kick back, crack open a beer and enjoy the ride.

Oh we wish.

The 40th floor comes with its own pressures and any thoughts of living the good life are soon left at the gate. When we live on our own floor separate from the news journalists, we enjoy a relatively unruffled existence. Not only are we focused on features, which are less time-sensitive and therefore less stressful than news, but being marginalized in out-of-the-way offices is something of a blessing. We're left alone to do our thing. We have a table tennis table and a Nintendo Wii. We fill the fridge with beer, gin and tonic to make what late nights we work pass easier. But thankfully there aren't too many of those. Several of the staff turn up to work at 10am, though the official start is 9am, and Demaria turns a blind eye. Life is easy.

Up on the 40th, I don't think I'm the only one who spends a moment or two wondering how the busy veterans in news will perceive us. On top of this, just prior to our move, CNN undergoes a massive rebranding under the recently appointed head, Jeff Zucker, that again forces the more strategically tuned of us to question if we really have been accepted into the CNN fold as fully as we believe.

The new direction under Zucker redirects the CNN focus back to hard news. Over the last few years CNN has reached away from this core essential, with lifestyle and other non-news features. Zucker wants to get back to news and he wants to do it primarily on TV. Certain programs are cut and staff laid off. Zucker's only trip to Hong Kong since he takes over in January 2013 is 20 months later, the week we move onto the 40th floor, and it's a political one, designed to throw a personal touch over the imminent layoffs. Three hundred people - 8 percent of CNN Worldwide - are cut in the last few months of 2014 as Zucker announces he's returning CNN to its core strength. The slogan is changed from "The most trusted name in news" to "Go there" and daubed over floors and walls and elevator doors to remind all of us inside what our mission now is.

It's another message that we don't quite fit, that while travel is all about 'going there', we'll never be able to relax, never be fully integrated into the inner circle of indispensable CNN departments.

Within a week of moving to the 40th floor, I leave.

I'd actually handed my notice in six weeks before, having been approached by another startup-like media enterprise to lead their digital operations. I'm walking to lunch when the call comes in. "Mr. James Durston?" asks a soft female voice.

"Yes."

"Mr. James, I am Ada for recruitment firm X, and I have a client who is looking for someone of your talent and experience to join their exciting new venture."

A couple of interviews and an offer with a 40% salary hike later, I decide the CNN ride has to come to a halt and it's time to explore something fresh.

I'm surprisingly nervous walking into Andrew Demaria's office to let him know. I buy a chocolate bar and slide it to him across the desk as I sit down, a kind of peace offering to say, "it's not personal, and it'll all be ok". That may sound self-important, but just a couple weeks earlier another editor on the team hands in her notice and Demaria appears flustered, if only by the knowledge that he now has to rejig staff and rearrange resources. I also know that I've been responsible for many of the biggest traffic stories on the site and losing your biggest traffic generator, just as I did earlier when one of my major writers was blacklisted, is always going to cause a headache, even if you also know they can easily be replaced.

He, being far more emotionally mature than I am,

147

handles the news easily and with grace. The only sticking point comes a few days later when he wants to confirm my exit date and we clash on how much of my three-month notice period I should serve. But we work it out, and a week after moving to the newsroom, I'm out.

I get a Photoshopped version of the CNN Travel homepage with fake headlines and pics, as has been the tradition for the last few years when someone departs. These things are a joy, masterpieces of loving abuse summing up the professional years prior. They're soaked through with the voice we used to express, and I spend a good ten minutes reading mine thoroughly, often laughing out loud to some of the burns. Some examples:

"THIS FUCKING BULLSHIT NEVER HAPPENED AT POTATO PROCESSING INTERNATIONAL!

"Former spuds diva* and 'Best Beaches' pimp decries lack of journalistic integrity in yet another boozy late-night email tirade aimed at CNN bosses."

(*Yes, I used to work for a magazine called Potato Processing International)

"As editorial enabler moves on, Google-dependent list churners around world suddenly out of favor at CNN"

"You fucking fuckhead. Flatter the boss the right way"

"PARLAYING AN ANTI-SOCIAL PERSONALITY INTO CAREER ADVANCEMENT

"Advocate for smog, panda extinction, museum

closures and staying at home lands job with new media group"

I know I'm leaving behind a great job and some great people. But the question marks that hang over CNN Travel, the promise of a fresh start on something brand new and a helpful salary hike combine to force my decision. When you feel like you're stagnating, you've got to get out of the pond.

As it happens my concerns for CNN Travel are not entirely unfounded. While it still appears to be running strong today (November 2016), with content and social media activity going up every day, there are even fewer staff. Voluntary departures and yet another round of redundancies sees just one original CNNGoer remain. There are just three content people dedicated to Travel now, not including those in the US. Chuck Thompson himself is the most recent 'removal' at the time of this writing. The freelance budget still exists, but it's shrunk, and perhaps is still shrinking.

It's not too great a stretch to suggest CNN Travel and CNNGo have been victims of their own success - or at least, the staff have. CNNGo's mission at the start, albeit vague and undefined, is to prove there's an audience for some kind of lifestyle content CNN is not yet producing on a grand scale. And we do it, becoming a travel site.

But now we have business goals to hit and a transition is needed, with a rebranding into CNN Travel, greater reach, a softer voice and more advertiser-friendly persona. That allows CNN Travel to grow, become profitable and establish itself among the world's best-read travel content platforms. It passes a critical mass and can afford to start shedding ballast. That ballast being the content producers that got it this far.

This isn't a complaint. If news can be a business, travel lifestyle content can certainly be a business. And it should be. From September 2009 to October 2016, I roughly guesstimate CNNGo/Travel has paid out US$700-800,000 to freelancers, and that's only because it's run as a business. Those of us lucky enough to see it all happening from the inside get a glimpse of how a startup develops, mutates, grows and establishes itself, all of it guided by the commercial carrot: do what you want, but you have to make money.

Sound advice for freelancers too.

23 A RAMBLING ESSAY-ISH CHEAT SHEET TO PITCHING

Hopefully by now you have a good idea of what goes into a buyable pitch, and have picked up a few insights into the life of a travel editor that can inform your queries.

Here are a few other things in no particular order to consider in your initial pitch.

Devices
Don't be afraid to pitch device-specific. Mobile will soon be, if not already in some regions, bigger than desktops for web traffic. If you have an idea for a story that for whatever reason would work great on mobile - flag this up. Many publishers are now thinking 'mobile first' and have the ability to select stories for specific devices, or at least are aware of and keen to prioritize the mobile side of their business.

Style guides
Ask for a style guide. It shows you're serious and want to provide good copy.

Offer everything
Don't be entitled. Offer anything and everything that you think might help get you the job; pictures, extra interviews, extra research, whatever. It'll also help you get the next job.

Subject line
Your email subject line is important. Don't sound PRish or spammy. Something like: "Freelancer pitch: 10 ways to guarantee your email is read" is fine. It lets me know this is from a writer, not a PR, and I immediately see the hook.

Don't forget the story
Don't think it ends with the pitch. It's always disappointing when you get a great pitch and a sloppy story. And that happens often. The best content entices with a great headline and delivers with an excellent feature. A great head without a great 'body' is just clickbait, a great body with a poor head won't get clicked.

Are you famous?
Probably the single best way to ensure your pitch gets read and considered seriously is to be a famous writer. The second best way is to meet your chosen editor first. The third best way is to get an introduction. Not from a fellow writer who once pitched an editor (and never heard back). But from someone who knows the editor personally and

whose opinion they trust. This means networking, going to writerly events, sticking out your hand and engaging the editor (or the editor's friend) in interesting conversation, maybe even discussing your ideas then, which have already been thoroughly researched and you know are appropriate for the editor's publication - basically showing that you are a pro and someone to be taken seriously. The fourth best way is to have an absolute nut of a story that no one else has, and to pitch it properly.

Quality vs. quantity
You might think that pitching two-dozen stories to an editor means at least one will get their attention and pique their curiosity. It's not entirely untrue. I have assigned pieces before simply due to the effort put in by the writer in the pitch. One "pitch" I received came in the form of a printed booklet, with pretty pictures and graphics, detailing a dozen or so stories that were ready and waiting to be bought. It was kind of a travel content brochure and after meeting the writer on his way through Hong Kong, assigned a couple of pieces to him.

But your time is far better spent getting good stories, finding interesting angles and pitching well. The impression you leave, of someone capable of doing good work (a pro), will be worth it even if a sale doesn't immediately occur.

How long?
Pitch length is something I know writers wrestle with. How short is too short? How long is too long? I prefer short pitches that expand as I read down. Refer back to

Chapter 5 and the fifth worst pitch I ever received: more than 1,000 words and then followed up, in the same day, with a 300-word "sorry can I just add ..." No! Stop! Think about your own feelings, when an editor sends you a style guide 65 pages long, in nine-point font, italicized. Far better to get a two-page document just summing up the main points, isn't it? That's what I send out to freelancers, and I expect similarly concise pitches in return.

Head first

If it wasn't already clear, ALWAYS START WITH A POTENTIAL HEADLINE. Then a few words, that could be the standfirst/dek/sub-head/sell (whatever you like to call it). Then an expansion, possibly the first par of the story. Finally a wrap-up of who else you will talk to and what other angles or points the piece will cover.

If you don't have this distilled quality to your pitch, I can't be sure you know the story too well yourself. Which may be ok - maybe part of the story is a discovery, something you don't know yet. But if you're pitching a done deal, you need to be able to sum it up and boil it down, so I know in clear terms exactly what it's about and I know you know that too.

The writing

Your writing within your pitch really does matter. You may even have a mediocre idea, but if I think your voice, style, sense of humor, or other writing qualities I see in my inbox could help it sing, I may well be tempted to assign. Needless to say typos, names spelled wrong, calling CNN

Travel CNNGo two years after it transformed (happened several times) won't necessarily plunge your pitch into the dark abyss of the trash bin, but it makes it ten times more likely.

Be human

You have to get inside the head of your editor and realize just how many shitty pitches he or she probably has to deal with on a weekly, if not daily basis. You may wonder why the hell most editors never send a response ("How difficult is it just to send a simple, 'thanks but no thanks'? I mean really..."), but for some it's like making eye contact with the beggar - suddenly he latches on, his eye won't let you go, he's there, looking at you, and suddenly he's talking to you, and you just want to walk to the store to get a pack of hedgehog flavored chips and bottle of gin, and you wonder why oh why did I make eye contact, I knew this would happen, it pains me it really does, but no, you cannot have my dollar and you should know you've just ruined it for every other beggar in this city who likes to make eye contact, because I will never look at another beggar again in my life. Until the next time, of course.

Many editors won't send even the most cursory of responses to a doomed pitch because often it just invites more doomed pitches, and most editors don't have the time or the masochistic qualities to want to do that. It may be infuriating, but that's how this game works, and boiling yourself up into an angry froth that explodes into a venomous email isn't going to do you any favors.

Be the best

Also remember I want the best. So explaining superfluous (self-oriented) reasons about why you're pitching (I'm just getting back into the game, I want to expand my audience, urrghh!) may be honest, but it's not what I want to hear. You need to sell your story and yourself.

EPILOGUE

It's been two and a bit years since I left CNN Travel for a job that made the ups and downs of self-doubt and success at CNN look positively benign. Ada from recruitment company X sold me on a gig at LE PAN, a brand new, super-ambitious, well-funded fine wine and luxury lifestyle magazine. I joined as digital director, to develop and launch their website and an app. As well as wine it would cover travel, food, design, fashion and other topics of glamour and desire. About two weeks ago from the time of this writing (November 2016) I quit that job too, after two years and three months at the digital helm, with a huge sigh of relief.

There's no room to go into detail here about that experience (there may even be another short book in it!), but I learned a few things I'll put down here, with the hope that should you, dear reader, encounter these in the future, I will at least be able to say "Well I warned you!"

- If a manager tells you there are no financial goals, no traffic or circulation targets, no ad revenue goals and no plans to introduce any in the future, don't believe him or her. At the very least, don't believe this means the publication will forever be given free access to a large budget without compromises.
- Try as hard as you can to skill yourself up for digital publishing and writing.
- High paydays rarely last. Make the most of them when you can.
- Be aware that no good thing lasts forever. A nice office, in a nice location, with nice people and a grand plan to produce one of the world's best magazines can easily and quickly become a shitty office in a shitty location with people getting laid off and a product that is progressively less ambitious.
- But don't burn bridges.

I'm now one week into my new job: digital editor at an agency leading the launch of an exciting new travel content website for Cathay Pacific. Already I'm becoming aware of some differences between the consumer-facing and client-incumbent sides of this trade. But my aim is pretty much the same as it has always been over the last ten years - to create great travel content online.

I'd be happy to engage with any writers who've read this far - connect with me on LinkedIn if you haven't already (https://hk.linkedin.com/in/jamesdurston) or head to my blog (travelwriteearn.com) and sign up to the newsletter to keep up to date with my thoughts on travel writing as a career.

And of course, if you have a great story, with an irresistible angle, described in a pitch that is succinct, organized and headlined, send it to me.

READ NEXT

Look out for the next books in the Travel Write Earn series:

Freelance Travel Writing
50 Most Important Questions Answered
A travel editor answers freelancer questions about selling, pitching, conceiving and writing travel stories (expected price: US$0.99-2.99)

What Editors Want
The Other Side Of The Email Divide
A travel editor sheds an insightful light on how a travel desk at a major media organization works (expected price: free)

Follow James Durston on twitter: @jedurston
Follow his blog: www.travelwriteearn.com

Made in United States
Orlando, FL
11 June 2023

34035108R00104